D1532121

Comfort Me
with Offal

Ruth Bourdain's Guide to Gastronomy

Ruth Bourdain

**Andrews McMeel
Publishing, LLC**

Kansas City • Sydney • London

Comfort Me with Offal copyright © 2012 by Ruth Bourdain. All rights reserved. Printed in the United States of America. No part of this book may be used or reproduced in any manner whatsoever without written permission except in the case of reprints in the context of reviews.

Andrews McMeel Publishing, LLC
an Andrews McMeel Universal company
1130 Walnut Street, Kansas City, Missouri 64106

www.andrewsmcmeel.com

Book design by Mike Miller
Illustrations by Matthew Endersbe

12 13 14 15 16 RR2 10 9 8 7 6 5 4 3 2 1
ISBN: 978-1-4494-2748-1
Library of Congress Control Number: 2012936744

This book is a parody of *Comfort Me with Apples: More Adventures at the Table*, Ruth Reichl's book about her adventures cooking and eating (and more) with great chefs of the world. *Comfort Me with Offal* is from Ruth Bourdain, the popular Twitter personality, who can also be found at comfortmewithoffal.com. Neither Ruth Reichl nor Anthony Bourdain was involved in writing, producing, or marketing this book; they are not affiliated in any way with the publisher or author of the book; and neither of them has endorsed the book or any of its contents. *Bonne lecture.*

ATTENTION: SCHOOLS AND BUSINESSES
Andrews McMeel books are available at quantity discounts with bulk purchase for educational, business, or sales promotional use. For information, please e-mail the Andrews McMeel Publishing Special Sales Department: specialsales@amuniversal.com

FOR PORK

"Animals are limited in their taste; some live only on vegetables, others on flesh; others feed altogether on grain; none know anything of composite flavors.

"Man is omnivorous. All that is edible is subjected to his vast appetite, a thing which causes gustatory powers proportionate to the use he has to make of them. The apparatus of taste is a rare perfection of man and we have only to see him use it to be satisfied of it."

Jean Anthelme Brillat-Savarin, The Physiology of Taste

Table of Contents

Introduction   x

Prologue: "From Macarons to Marrow"   xii

CHAPTER 1: A Brief History of Gastronomy   1

A time line of highs and lows in food history, from prehistoric times to the birth of the modern era

    "Ruthie & Julia"   2

    The History of Gastronomy: A Time Line   4

CHAPTER 2: Carniwhores, Gastrosexuals, and Curd Nerds: A Field Guide to the Modern Foodie   15

A typology of the varied species of food obsessives whom you may encounter in your culinary journeys

    "A Brave New World"   16

    A Field Guide to the Modern Foodie   17

CHAPTER 3: Navigating the Edible Industrial Complex   41

Explorations of the contemporary world of food, including the rise of the celebrity chef, food trends, understanding restaurant criticism, and how to communicate with waiters

    "El Bulli Death Trip"   42

    The Rise of the Celebrity Chef   44

    So You Want to Be a . . . Celebrity Chef   57

    Trend Mapping: A Food Trend's Journey   58

    Breastaurants: Boom or Bust?   61

    How to Read a Restaurant Review   62

    So You Want to Be a . . . Restaurant Critic   68

    Deciphering the Menu   70

    How to Deal with Waiters   70

    Etiquette Points: The Art of Eating with Others   72

    Restaurant-Speak Decoded   78

    Culinary Travels: "That's Not My Risotto" and Other Local
       Food Idioms   79

    How to Survive a Vegan Apocalypse   86

CHAPTER 4: The Gastronomical Me   89

How to be a gastronome, including understanding basic culinary anatomy and how to train your mind, body, and palate to optimize your gastronomical pleasure points

"A Zest for Life"	90
Food 101: Introduction to Culinary Anatomy	92
Exercising Your Palate: Five Simple Techniques to Bulk Up Your Taste Buds	98
So You Want to Be a . . . Food Memoirist	100
Culinary Code: A Guide to Food Acronyms	102
Mind, Body, Palate: Gastro-Yoga with Rick Bayless	104
The Joy of Cooking: A Culinary Kama Sutra	106
The Art of Getting Gastrostoned	112
On Parenting: Raising a Gastronome	114
A Basic Guide to Portion Size	118
Me, MyPlate, and I	122

CHAPTER 5: Matters of Taste   127

Lessons in food and flavor, from cheese to chocolate, herbs, and meat

"Down and Out in London"	128
Cup This: How to Taste Coffee	130
Cutting the Cheese	134
All about Meat	136
Herbs for Seasoning and for Smoking	140
Pasta 2.0: New Pasta Shapes	142
So You Want to Be a . . . Hipster Butcher	150
Food-Safety Checklist	151
Holiday Cooking Tips: Be a Master Baster	152
Orgasmic Chocolate: From Foreplay to Climax	154
You Are What You Eat	155
Should You Eat That Chicken? A Decision-Making Flowchart	159

CHAPTER 6: The World of Wine and Spirits   161

The essentials of tasting wine and spirits, understanding the language of wine-speak, and pairing wine with food

"How I Learned to Stop Worrying and Love Hedonistic
   Fruit Bombs"   162

How to Taste a Glass of Wine   163

An Introduction to Wine–Speak   168

Wine Words: A Cheat Sheet   170

The Art of Wine Pairing   172

So You Want to Be a . . . Wine Critic   173

That's the Spirit: A Guide to the Hard Stuff   174

Some Sex on the Beach Variations   178

Cocktail Lingo: A Cheat Sheet   179

APPENDIX: What's Your GQ?   181

Take this simple questionnaire to find your gastronomical quotient (GQ), which measures your culinary knowledge, gastronomical prowess, and gustatory morality

Acknowledgments   191

Introduction

Thank you for purchasing *Comfort Me with Offal: Ruth Bourdain's Guide to Gastronomy*, the most important contribution to food writing since Jean Anthelme Brillat-Savarin's *The Physiology of Taste*. Now that you have acquired this book, you may go ahead and throw away your copy of that other one (or, to be "green," you may recycle it in a special bin now available at your local Whole Foods Market). But don't get rid of all your food reference books: You will still need to hold on to your mammoth copy of *Larousse Gastronomique* (it comes in very handy for step aerobics).

Thirty-five years ago, over a memorable dinner in Chinatown, the legendary James Beard told me, "Ruth, you must write this book." Now, he did have his mouth full of chicken feet at the time, and his speech was slurred from smoking way too much tarragon, so there is a good possibility he might have actually said, "Ruth, you must try this *jook*," referring to the rice porridge he was eating (it was amazing). Nevertheless, I'm still pretty sure he encouraged me to put pen to paper and at long last share my deep knowledge of gastronomy with the entire universe.

While *Comfort Me with Offal* may be more than three decades in the making, it represents the first and only comprehensive guide to our current state of gastronomy. And there couldn't be a better time for an instruction manual for the world of food. Let's face it: The culinary world has gotten a little confusing as of late. Is bagged salad clean and safe to eat? What the fuck is "air-chilled chicken," anyway? And what's up with Padma Lakshmi? Is she stoned on *Top Chef*? Unfortunately, this book does not contain the answers to any of those questions, but it will equip you with the basic knowledge of gastronomy so that you can search for the answers on your own.

We start in Chapter 1, "A Brief History of Gastronomy," with a look back at the history of food and its eaters and how we evolved from the most ancient culinarians to the modern-day Yelper.

Chapter 2 provides a "Field Guide to the Modern Foodie," an essential guide to the diverse and eclectic types of food obsessives—from carniwhores to gastrosexuals—who comprise the contemporary food world.

Chapter 3, "Navigating the Edible Industrial Complex," explores the current state of gastronomy, including the rise of the celebrity chef, the importance of celebrity chef hair (or lack thereof), and lucrative new frontiers in pharmaceutical endorsements for top chefs; food trends; how to read a restaurant review; and etiquette points for eating with others. In this day and age, it's critical to think about food choices, so we'll also explore some tips and techniques for managing portion size and preparing for the eventuality of a vegan apocalypse.

In Chapter 4, "The Gastronomical Me," we'll turn to the eater as animal, studying its basic anatomy and the steps humans can take to hone their gustatory abilities. You'll learn about the joy of cooking (culinary sex!) and the art of getting gastrostoned.

Finally, in Chapter 5, "Matters of Taste," we get to the food (that is, meat, cheese, coffee, and chocolate). You've probably never tasted any of those things, so this will be a vital resource, which pairs nicely with Chapter 6, "The World of Wine and Spirits," where we might get a little bit drunk (please appoint a designated driver while reading this important chapter).

At the end of the book, I've included a quiz—What's Your Gastronomical Quotient (GQ)?—a standardized tool for assessing your knowledge of food and aptitude for all things culinary.

Throughout this volume, I've collected some memorable stories from my own personal history in the world of food and wine, along with my rules ("Ruth's Rules") for eating, which Michael Pollan shamelessly ripped off in his *Food Rules* book. "So You Want to Be a..." questionnaires will assess your aptitude for culinary careers as a celebrity chef, restaurant critic, sommelier, and more.

I hope that this guide will become as cherished as your well-worn copy of *Mastering the Art of French Cooking*. I think Julia Child would have wanted it that way.

Bon Appétit!

Prologue

"From Macarons to Marrow"

July 1966
PARIS, France

I woke up in the Luxembourg Gardens just as dawn was breaking, the sunlight ever so slightly caramelizing the crust of sugar and egg whites on my lips.

I sat up, licked my lips, and tasted almonds and vanilla. I shrugged and fell back into the wet grass as a group of schoolgirls paraded by, looking down at me with a combination of fear and disgust.

I was strung out on macarons. I spent the night before binging at Dalloyau, Ladurée, and who the hell knows where else. It was all one big blur. In fact, I could barely remember anything that happened.

There was something stuck in my bra. Was that a bouchon?

I reached down to scratch my ass and discovered a crushed cannelle. How the hell did that get there?

I had really hit rock bottom. I was supposed to be in Paris on assignment for Pastrygirl *magazine, writing an article on the city's best patisseries. But before long, I found myself spiraling into a pastry addiction. I was turning into a junkie, and it was taking its toll.*

And now, here I was, fucked up on sweets and all alone in Luxembourg Gardens. It was pathetic.

But while it may have been my lowest point, it was also the moment when everything changed for me. Because that was when I met François, the man who transformed my life forever.

I don't know what he saw in me, this broken-down wreck of a person covered in macaron crumbs with various pastries protruding from my undergarments. But we looked at each other from across the park and immediately locked eyes. He started right toward me: a big, strapping Frenchman on a unicycle. At first, he rode toward me at top speed, swerving around the schoolgirls, grinding tulips beneath his tire. And then he leapt right off the unicycle and started running—sprinting, actually—right toward me until he dived into the grass.

He rolled over right next to me.

It was a little scary to feel magnetism this strong, but it was mutual. He didn't speak a word of English, but with his hand gestures and my rudimentary French, we started to communicate in a primordial fashion. He motioned to his backpack, pulled it off his broad shoulders, and dropped it to the ground. It made a resounding thud from something heavy inside. What was it?

He unbuckled the top and pulled out a lobe of foie gras. He held the giant engorged liver up to my lips, but I looked away. I was still a vegetarian at that time, if you can believe it. But he grabbed me by the chin and pulled my head toward his.

"Mangez," he commanded in a soft, raspy voice.

"No," I told him. "I don't eat meat."

Unconvinced, he told me, again, to eat the foie gras.

I don't know what came over me, but I did as I was told.

I sunk my teeth right into the foie. And then he grabbed me and pulled me to him and we kissed, an amazing and unforgettable emulsion of European saliva, unfiltered cigarettes, animal fat, and macarons from last night's binge.

Somehow, he uncorked a bottle of Côtes du Rhône using his furry bare hands and gave me a swig to wash everything down. It was a taste memory I will never, ever forget. And from that day forward, I would never call myself a vegetarian again.

It was a whirlwind. He strapped his unicycle to the top of his Citroën and drove me straight to the Marché International de Rungis, the wholesale meat market. I silently watched—gawked, really—as I saw François in action bargaining with the purveyors for meat. His arms waved madly. Sometimes he shouted. Other times he whispered. Transactions were made. Cash was exchanged. He bought cuts of meat and organs I had never heard of before. The flesh came in stunning shades of red, ruby, and purple. And, it came from animals whose names mystified:

German horsecow, Lithuanian fishgoat, Alsatian rabbit-eared lamb, and an incredible oddity called an Iberico pig-tailed chicken.

Somehow, he stuffed the incredible bounty of meats into the trunk of the Citroën, and we sped from market to market, filling the broken-down car with even more incredible food: cheeses that smelled like farts, the freshest fruits and vegetables, wine, and fatty charcuterie.

He took me back to his apartment. We trudged up the steep, creaky stairs with our gastronomic loot to the top floor. When we made it there, he lifted me up with his burly arms, carried me through the doorway, and tossed me onto the bed. I closed my eyes, shimmied out of my clothes, and waited for him to join me. But he didn't. Before long, I heard the sounds of him cooking madly in the kitchen: bones breaking, pans crashing, pepper grinding, flesh tearing, sinew sinewing. And the smells—they were simply intoxicating. I got up to join him, but he motioned at me to sit back down.

"Asseyez-vous," he yelled from the kitchen.

OK, OK, I said to myself, and got back in bed.

I must have fallen asleep, because the next thing I knew, François was back, and all of the food was cooked.

And we sat in bed as he fed me things I had never tasted.

In his best broken English, he told me, "We must eat from zee nose to zee tail."

And so we did. There were cheeks, snouts, ears, even chins. Then we moved on to the shoulders, ribs, loins, and organ meats. He juggled thymus glands of various breeds and then popped them into my mouth. We shared a braised beef heart, gnawing at it together. We bobbed for foie gras in a vat full of absinthe. He whipped me with lambs' intestines and massaged me with lardo. And you know what? I loved it. And I wanted to let him know.

"This is so incredibly unctuous," I told him after happily taking a bite of fatty braised pork belly.

He frowned and wagged his finger.

"I'm sorry," I said. "It's just so good. I love the mouthfeel."

"Non!" he yelled curtly.

"Um, OK," I said. "It's really 'to die for'?"

"Jamais!" he yelled, exasperated.

"How about 'toothsome'?"

"Non!"

"Delish?"

"Merde!!"

"Yummy?"

"Ta gueule!" he shot back, using the French slang for "shut up."

"Listen, François," I cried. "I just want you to know how fucking good this shit is!"

"Parfait! Parfait! Très bien!" he shouted. This time, he was pleased. He smiled, beaming at me. Struggling with English, he whispered, "In this way—how do you say—you will not be une douchebaguette."

What a dick, I thought. But he was right. All I knew were clichéd food terms. It was a revelation. To this day, I have never uttered the word "toothsome" again.

Later, after clearing the bed of our dinner, François came back to the bedroom with a bottle of absinthe and two straws. We dispensed with the ritual of pouring the liquor over sugar, and sipped it together. Before long, I hallucinated that I was inside a pig eating my way out. It was as disturbing as it was delicious. And then I must have fallen asleep, because I woke up the next morning in a pile full of half-chewed meat parts and aioli smeared all over my body.

It didn't take long for me to realize that François was gone, and I was all alone. He left behind a note that he was married, that he could never see me again, and that I should pack my things and go before he returned that evening. I burst into tears and collapsed into the bed, sucking on marrow bones as my only solace.

CHAPTER 1

A Brief History
of Gastronomy

A time line of highs and lows in food history,
from prehistoric times to the birth of the modern era

"Ruthie & Julia"

October 1975
CAMBRIDGE, Massachusetts

Joining Julia Child for dinner was always an "interesting" experience. She was one of the few women—or men, for that matter—who could drink me under the table, and her enthusiasm for cooking, food, and culinary technique was incredibly infectious. Speaking of infectious, I'm pretty sure I caught something one time when she cooked me boeuf Bourguignon at her house in Cambridge.

In all my years, I'll never forget watching, in stomach-turning horror, as she proceeded to drop nearly every ingredient in the recipe on the floor as she cooked (and continued to cook).

"There go the onions!" she exclaimed as they rolled off the counter. She bolted after them, gathering them up with her long arms. But as she swung back around to get her chef's knife and begin chopping, her hips knocked four pounds of raw meat off the counter.

"Oh, drat! That's going to be a problem, isn't it?" she said as we both watched the beef flop from the counter down to the floor, landing on one of her husband Paul's slippers.

"You're probably not going to believe me now, but you know I never dropped a turkey on live television," she confided.

I rolled my eyes. Sure you didn't, I thought to myself.

"Don't worry about it," she said. "We'll just carry on. That's why they call it the thirty-second rule, don't they?"

"You mean the five-second rule?" I asked.

"Give or take twenty-five seconds," she replied with a wink and a half-smile. "It's nothing a little butter can't fix."

Oh, Jesus, I thought.

And then, just as we had scraped all of the meat off the floor and removed the dust, she dropped the bottle of burgundy. It would have been comical were it not for the fact that she continued to cook with all the fallen foodstuffs. I excused myself to the bathroom to raid her medicine cabinet for antibiotics.

"Don't worry, Ruth! It happens all the time!" she called out to me as I came back down the hallway with a mouthful of Cipro. "When you're alone in the kitchen, who's going to see, anyway?" she said.

"But you're not alone, Julia," I mumbled as I swallowed the pills. "What about me? I'm here!" That minor detail seemed to escape her.

I offered to help clean up, but as I reached out to lend a hand, she dropped a stick of butter, slipped on an onion skin, and landed right in the puddle of wine, taking me down with her. The two of us were lying on the floor drenched in wine and cow's blood and smelling like onions.

"Isn't this a fine mess!" she chortled as she handed me a straw to sip the burgundy off the floor. "No thanks," I said as I threw up in my mouth a little.

THE HISTORY OF GASTRONOMY: A TIME LINE

How did we get here?

In the hustle and bustle of our modern times, always searching for the new "new," the latest food trend, and a reservation at one of Thomas Keller's restaurants, we can sometimes lose sense of our history. If you can believe it, not long ago, there were no gourmet food trucks, no panini sandwiches or *banh mi*, and even *sous-vide* machines were almost unheard of. In fact, just a couple of decades ago, man subsisted almost entirely on tuna tartare and molten chocolate cake. And before that, there was something called "tuna casserole." Those were the darkest of times.

Some have argued, profoundly, that the evolution of human beings and gastronomy went hand in hand. Grasping control of fire and using it as a means to cook (and smoke a pipe filled with tangerine zest or the drug of one's choice) may be the single most significant event in human evolution *and* culinary history. In many ways, perhaps we can call ourselves humans today only because of this critical moment in history: mastering fire. Think about it. With the exception of sushi, of course, without fire there would be no gastronomy as we know and cherish it: no braised short ribs, no bistecca alla Fiorentina, and no McRibs (OK, maybe fire's not such a good thing).

Anyway, to get some perspective on *Homo gastronomus* ("Gastro-Man") and trace his evolution into the modern foodie, it helps to take a look backward. What follows is a time line of some of the most significant events in food history, from the Prehistoric Era to the ancient world, the Middle Ages, and, finally, the birth of contemporary gastronomy as we know it today.

The Prehistoric Era

This is where it all started, before the advent of Microplane graters, the invention of the Cuisinart, or even the evolution of humans. Terrifying as it may sound, plant-eating dinosaurs—the planet's first vegans—ruled the Earth until the arrival of flesh eaters like *Tyrannosaurus rex,* which started one of the world's first global food trends: carrion. Not long afterward, early humans emerged. Woolly mammoth tartare was all the rage until the mastery of fire, when humans finally grasped the art of cooking. Our human ancestors might seem unrecognizable to us in many ways, but before long they would be making hollandaise sauce.

4.6 billion years ago
Earth opens for business, and it's hotter than ever (200 degrees Celsius, to be precise), though it would be billions of years until its first review appears on Yelp.

2.1 billion years ago
Eukaryotes, organisms whose cells contain complex structures enclosed within membranes, evolve. They are delicious served raw with a nice mignonette or simply a squeeze of lemon.

545 million years ago
Hard-shelled mollusks, the ancestors of snails, appear. Sadly, it would be many, many years until the invention of butter and the evolution of parsley.

225 million years ago
The dinosaurs emerge. Carrion is the big food trend in carnivorous dinosaur circles.

2.3 million years ago
The appearance of *Homo habilis,* the first "true human," occurs. He used stone tools to hunt and scavenge meat. Woolly mammoth tartare goes big-time.

1.8 million years ago
A skilled hunter, *Homo erectus* evolves. With his emergence, the Age of Prehistoric Sushi comes to a close as early man discovers how to use fire for cooking. Archaeologists name him *Homo bobbyflayus.*

200,000 years ago
Homo sapiens emerge, with all of the physical and anatomical features familiar to modern men and women, including the ability to *sous-vide.*

130,000 years ago
Neanderthals evolve. They almost become extinct 22,000 years ago, before reemerging in modern times in the form of Guy Fieri.

12,000 BC
People living on Egypt's Lower Nile use grinding stones to produce a kind of flour from the seeds of wild grasses. Their descendants will shop the bulk aisles at Whole Foods.

10,000 BC
Crude forms of flatbread are being made for the first time, though archaeologists cannot confirm whether this was the "original" Ray's pizza.

9,000 BC
Bows and arrows are used in Europe for hunting, though spears remain the most commonly used weapons. And yet, Microplane graters still don't exist.

6,500 BC
The wheel is invented in Sumer, radically changing transportation and setting forth the evolution of gourmet food trucks.

Ancient Epicureanism

The rise of civilizations stretching from Asia to Europe brought humans together into communities. Major advances took place in agriculture, husbandry, and social vomiting. Even so, it would be years until anyone could make a decent espresso.

490 BC
Pre-dating McDonald's, Persia's Darius I has one thousand animals slaughtered every day for the royal table in Persepolis.

350 BC
The first cookbook is written by Greek author Archestratus. Shortly thereafter, he is struck down by a lightning bolt from Zeus for publishing a recipe for vegan mayonnaise.

312 BC
An aqueduct connects Rome to springs outside the city, bringing fresh water to its inhabitants. Roman residents eagerly await the construction of a beerqueduct.

300 BC
Sugarcane from India is introduced into the Middle East, but "frosted falafel" never really takes off as a food trend.

100 BC
Romans begin to cultivate oysters in beds. While it's an effective form of early aquaculture, they also discover that it's extremely uncomfortable to sleep that way.

54 BC
Julius Caesar invades Britain, but never really gets the Marmite thing.

1 BC
At the Last Supper, a Passover seder, Jesus proclaims the matzo balls to be "a little on the dense side."

44
The vomitorium, an early ancestor of the buffet restaurant, is all the rage in Rome.

100
The first mechanical dough mixer is invented by Marcus Vergilius Eurysaces. It consists of a large stone basin with wooden paddles powered by a horse or donkey. While the dough mixer is hugely successful, his crude attempt at building a turtle-powered Slap Chop fails miserably.

273
In addition to a daily bread ration, Roman emperor Aurelianus adds pork fat to the list of foods distributed free to the populace. Man, those were the days.

408
The Visigoths attack Rome, and demand three thousand pounds of pepper as ransom. The epic race to invent the first pepper grinder begins in earnest.

827
Spinach is introduced into Sicily by the Saracens, pissing off Sicilian kids no end.

833
Rulers in China forbid the population from drinking wine on days of national mourning. Naturally, they turn to the hard stuff.

850
According to legend, coffee is discovered by the Arab goatherd Kaidi when his goats get twitchy after chewing on raw coffee beans. The next morning, the goats experience headaches. Restless, they grunt their desire for cappuccinos.

Medieval and Renaissance Gastronomy

One of the darkest periods in human history occurs when the Goths invade Rome, bringing about an abrupt and brutal end to the Roman Empire. After Rome is sacked, it would be centuries until you could find a decent prosciutto. The world was riven by wars. Plagues decimated populations, and famine became one of the biggest food trends, not to mention gruel and mutton. But mostly famine.

907
A cataclysmic turn of events for mankind: Tofu becomes popular in China.

1250
European crusaders return from the Middle East, bringing with them cardamom, cinnamon, cloves, coriander, cumin, saffron, and the worst hummus breath.

1492
Italian explorer Christopher Columbus discovers the New World, and opens up a chain of failed pizza restaurants.

1494
Columbus lands on the shores of Jamaica, logs on to Chowhound.com, and proclaims the jerk chicken to be the best he's ever had.

1561
Marmalade is invented by a physician to Mary Queen of Scots to settle her stomach. She later banishes him after his failure to heal her sprained ankle with apricot jam.

1582
The first mention of coffee occurs in print by a European merchant traveling to Arabia: "Jesus, this coffee sucks ass. Why does Starbucks always have to burn it?"

1621
Pilgrims and Native Americans celebrate their first Thanksgiving, a historic event in American history representing an important coming together and breaking of bread. Both groups find common ground in pledging to eat less the next year.

1634
To maintain the quality of its mustard, France imposes strict rules on mustard makers. A democratic movement in favor of ketchup emerges in response.

1681
The pressure cooker is invented. Thousands seek psychological help to deal with their deep-seated fears that the devices will explode in their kitchens.

1729
In "A Modest Proposal," Jonathan Swift advocates eating children to solve the Irish population crisis. Not a bad idea.

1762
To great success, the Earl of Sandwich invents the sandwich.

His longtime competitor, the Earl of Panini, is absolutely devastated and driven to depression.

1764
The first public restaurant opens in France. People are surprised the owners went with a Tex-Mex theme.

1774
English explorer James Cook nearly dies of poisoning after eating a blowfish. The seafood chain Red Blowfish quickly files for bankruptcy, shuttering all of its restaurants.

1784
Marie-Antoine Carême is born in Paris, France. Though considered by historians to be the world's first "celebrity chef," he is never selected to appear as a contestant on *Top Chef Masters*. What's up with that?

1850
One of the most horrifying days in food history: The American Vegetarian Society is established.

1870
Le Gourmet, a popular Parisian gastronomic journal, ceases publication. People debate whether the rise of blogs or the decline in luxury advertising was the cause of its downfall.

The Modern Era

We've come a long way since the evolution of *Homo bobbyflayus*. For the modern eater, the eternal quest for fire has evolved into the ultimate quest for umami. As food became industrialized, a new class of critics emerged who questioned the safety and sustainability of food systems. Many heeded their call, promoting organic, local, and seasonal foods, while others largely ignored them, unable to resist the siren song of In-N-Out Burger.

1903
A very chubby, bald baby is born who smells strangely of tarragon. His parents name him James Beard.

1908
Dr. Kikunae Ikeda of Tokyo Imperial University introduces the concept of umami, the so-called fifth taste that represents savoriness. People have absolutely no clue what he is talking about (and still don't).

1915
A devastating day for drinking: Absinthe is outlawed in France.

1920
Prohibition begins, and "bathtub gin" is born, along with the lesser known "toilet bourbon," which never really took off.

1924
A chef in Tijuana claims to have created the first-ever Caesar salad. The same guy also claims he created the hamburger, fettucine alfredo, paella, and the Waldorf salad. He is later executed in a public hanging and pelted with anchovies, garlic, and Parmesan cheese.

1929
The Dow Jones plummets, setting forth the Great Depression. Soup is suddenly the new hotness.

1933
Prohibition laws are repealed. Cheers!

1937
SPAM is invented. To this day, nobody knows what it's made of.

1938
Larousse Gastronomique, an important culinary reference book and doorstop, is published.

1954
"Broasted chicken" appears, to the confusion of the masses, who wonder, is it baked, roasted, broiled, boiled, or all four? The debate rages on to this day.

1955
Ray Kroc opens his first McDonald's burger stand and plots his world empire.

1956
Chef, restaurateur, and hotelier Alain Ducasse is born. In a first, his amniotic fluid is rated three Michelin stars.

1961
Julia Child publishes *Mastering the Art of French Cooking*. But concerns about her influence are raised after news reports that many Americans are overdosing on boeuf Bourguignon.

1969
Funyuns, a packaged onion-flavored snack food, are introduced, a godsend to stoners everywhere.

1971
Alice Waters puts peaches on a plate and serves it to unsuspecting rubes at her so-called restaurant Chez Panisse.

1974
Mama Cass Elliot of The Mamas & the Papas dies in London. Contrary to rumors, she did not choke to death on a ham sandwich. She choked to death on three ham sandwiches.

1978
Chef Jeremiah Tower leaves Chez Panisse. On his way out, Alice Waters angrily eggs him with an organic, free-range, wood fire—roasted egg.

1979
The first Zagat restaurant survey is published. The guide is considered "useful" to some, even if its descriptions can be "a little out of date" and the numerical ratings are "usually less than reliable."

1979
Celebrity chef Paul Prudhomme, a leader in Cajun cuisine, opens K-Paul's Louisiana Kitchen in New Orleans. Some find his "blackening up" of everything from catfish to chicken to be racially insensitive.

1982
The first California Pizza Kitchen opens. It's called "Spago."

1985
A tuna tartare epidemic ravages Los Angeles.

1987
Spanish chef Ferran Adrià takes over the kitchen of the restaurant El Bulli, bringing about revolutionary developments in the new field of molecular

gastronomy. Scarce reservations at the in-demand restaurant spawn a series of riots by foodies in world capitals.

1991
The last vestige of '80s cuisine, molten chocolate cake, appears, burning the tongues of millions worldwide.

1994
The Microplane rasp, invented in 1990 as a woodworking tool, is first used to zest an orange, and the era of narcotic citrus zesting and smoking begins.

1994
Bringing butter poaching to the masses, chef Thomas Keller opens The French Laundry in Yountville, California.

1995
The faddish cabbage soup diet, and the magnitude of result-ing farts from its adherents, is cited as a major man-made cause of global warming.

2003
America's first legal den of food porn opens in San Francisco. It's called the Ferry Building Marketplace.

2006
A major culinary invention, the deep-frying of Coca Cola, takes place.

2008
A landmark day for freedom in America: The USDA finally allows the import of *jamón Ibérico*.

2011
Pioneering molecular-gastronomy restaurant El Bulli closes. An explosion of first-person accounts of eating a final meal at the restaurant causes a global epidemic of El Boredom.

At a Glance: A Century of American Food Trends			
1910s	Prussian dressing	1960s	Old-fashioneds
1920s	Near beer	1970s	Fondue
1930s	Soup kitchens	1980s	Tuna tartare
1940s	War rations	1990s	Sun-dried tomatoes
1950s	Casseroles	2000s	Pork belly

HEAVEN AND HELL

The food world is a lot like *Star Wars:* there are the Jedis of gastronomy—heroic chefs, writers, and eaters who inspire us all—and then there are culinary Siths, a cult of madmen (and madwomen) hell-bent on destroying everything that is beautiful and delicious.

THE PANTHEON: The Jedi Knights of Gastronomy

Samuel Johnson (1709–1784)

WHO: English author, poet, editor, and lexicographer.

GASTRONOMIC GREATNESS: Feeding his beloved cat Hodge a diet of fresh-shucked oysters.

William the Conqueror (1028–1087)

WHO: The first Norman king of England.

GASTRONOMIC GREATNESS: After discovering he was too fat to ride his horse, he confined himself to bed and took up a liquid diet consisting entirely of alcoholic beverages.

Fergus Henderson (BORN 1963)

WHO: English chef, cookbook author, and restaurateur who founded the St. John restaurant in London.

GASTRONOMIC GREATNESS: Godlike proponent of "nose-to-tail eating" and the use of offal and other "nasty bits."

Mario Batali (BORN 1960)

WHO: Chef, restaurateur, and television personality whose restaurant empire stretches from Los Angeles to Singapore. Batali's signature (though questionable) fashion style includes shorts and orange Crocs.

GASTRONOMIC GREATNESS: Enhancing Americans' knowledge of regional Italian cuisines and spreading the gospel of guanciale *(cured hog's jowl) and* lardo *(cured pork fatback).*

Ljubomir Erovic (BORN 1963)

WHO: Serbian chef and testicle evangelist.

GASTRONOMIC GREATNESS: Founder of the annual "World Testicle & Aphrodisiac Cooking Championship," Erovic experienced an epicurean epiphany when he unwittingly devoured a delicious testicle goulash: "I couldn't sleep that very night because I became incredibly aroused and felt a real 'charge of positive energy' that I had to use somehow. I had never experienced anything like that before. The next day, after the wild night, I found out from a friend that the dish we ate was testicle goulash. I suddenly realized that it could be a great way to help the sexually troubled ones and through the cooking contests discover the strongest aphrodisiac to conquer the world."

Hannibal Lecter, MD (BORN 1933)

WHO: Brilliant psychiatrist, serial killer, and cannibal.

GASTRONOMIC GREATNESS: One of the leading advocates of eating people, Dr. Lecter is known especially for popularizing food and wine pairings such as "human liver with fava beans and a nice Chianti."

THE EVIL EMPIRE: The Sith Lords of Food

Jeff Smith (1939–2004)

WHO: The author of a dozen bestselling cookbooks, he was the host of The Frugal Gourmet *television cooking show on PBS from 1983 to 1997.*
CRIMES AGAINST GASTRONOMY: Cooking with Elmo.

Guy Fieri (BORN 1968)

WHO: Restaurateur, author, television personality, and game-show host, he co-owns five restaurants in California, and is one of the most popular cooking personalities on the Food Network.
CRIMES AGAINST GASTRONOMY: Flaming shirts, unbearable spiked hair, wearing sunglasses on the back of his head, extreme bastardization of food (he is responsible for such grotesque recipes as RITZ Cracker Cheesesteak Sliders), and general douchebaggery.

Alice Waters (BORN 1944)

WHO: Often called the "mother of American food," Waters is the pioneering chef and owner of Chez Panisse and a leading advocate of organic, locally grown ingredients.
CRIMES AGAINST GASTRONOMY: Pretentious habit of roasting eggs in a wood-fired oven for breakfast.

Rachael Ray (BORN 1968)

WHO: Husky-voiced television personality, celebrity chef, and cookbook author, she hosts a syndicated daytime talk show and several Food Network series. A glossy food magazine, Every Day with Rachael Ray, *bears her name.*
CRIMES AGAINST GASTRONOMY: Excessive perkiness; dumbing down the culinary arts and forever bastardizing food television; popularizing unbearable food words such as "Yumm-o" and the dreaded "E-V-O-O"; thirty-minute meals; creating and selling a "garbage bowl" for use during food prep.

Paula Deen (BORN 1947)

WHO: Cooking show host, restaurateur, author, and owner of The Lady & Sons restaurant in Savannah, Georgia, with her sons, Jamie and Bobby Deen.
CRIMES AGAINST GASTRONOMY: Doing unholy things with butter, deep-frying macaroni and cheese, inserting a burger between two Krispy Kreme doughnuts, and blinding the public with other unappealing culinary creations.

Graham Kerr (BORN 1934)

WHO: British television cooking personality and cookbook author famous for his Galloping Gourmet *show and persona.*
CRIMES AGAINST GASTRONOMY: Galloping.

CHAPTER 2

Carniwhores, Gastrosexuals, and Curd Nerds: A Field Guide to the Modern Foodie

*A typology of the varied species
of food obsessives whom you may encounter
in your culinary journeys*

"A Brave New World"

August 2008
SAN FRANCISCO, California

I woke up on the cold, hard floor of the Ferry Plaza Terminal Building with Cowgirl Creamery's Red Hawk cheese smeared across my face and a searing headache.

The sun was just rising, and the bright light shining in through the windows burned my eyes like a just-sliced habanero pepper on a baby's tongue. I was seriously hungover. How did I even get here? I must have had temporary amnesia.

As I sat up, I ran my fingers through my thick, curly hair and it felt wet and sticky. Oh Jesus. What the fuck! But then I smelled something sweet. I brought my fingers to my lips, licked them, and tasted the distinct flavor of Frog Hollow peaches. Damn, those really are some good peaches.

I stumbled out of the historic building into the farmers' market held outside, which was bustling with an enormous crowd of foodies. I was shocked to see so many of them, and they were all so diverse. Things had really changed since I first got started in the food world decades ago, when those few of us seriously interested in gastronomy seemed so small in number.

It was hard to take in. There were carniwhores in search of meaty sustenance, curd nerds seeking the calming effects of triple-crème cheese, locavores hunting down heirloom tomatoes, and then there were the dreaded vegans, who stared at me with their evil, darkened eyes shrouded in pale skin stretched over bone. A little coffeegeek sporting a beard and a wool hat (even though it was nearly eighty degrees) recognized me and brought me a quadruple espresso.

"You're Ruth Bourdain, right?" he said.

"I'm not really sure. I'm a little hungover and confused," I told him.

"Oh, you're definitely Ruth Bourdain. I'm a huge fan," said the coffeegeek as he turned around to show me his tramp stamp with my visage hovering just above his ass crack.

"Well, I guess I am," I said. "Yes. I guess I am."

A FIELD GUIDE TO THE MODERN FOODIE

Amuse-Douches: Scorned by FEMIVORES, these food dudes typically reside in "man caves," favor Ed Hardy shirts, and worship at the altar of dudeish chefs like Guy Fieri. Labeled also as FOUCHES in some circles, AMUSE-DOUCHES will only mate with DOUCHEBAGUETTES.

Artisinalarians: Deeply committed to hand made foods and traditional culinary techniques, they include both LOCAVORES and GLOBAVORES. ARTISANALARIANS are devoted to the demigod Alice Waters and follow the ritual of taking communion with an artisanal baguette spread with cultured European-style butter.

Barbecuties: Devotees of barbecue, BARBECUTIES are a loosely affiliated group of men and women bound by a common desire for smoked, slow-cooked meats. Like Catholics and Protestants in the Christian church, BARBECUTIES are divided into two major groups: the DRY RUBBERS, who prefer dry spice-rubbed barbecue, and the SAUCISTAS, who believe barbecue should be slathered with barbecue sauce. The confederation of BARBECUTIES includes splinter sects such as the KANSAS CITIZENS, MEMPHITES, and the Texan BRISKETEERS. A far-flung group of BARBECUTIES in China are known as the CHARSIUVIANS (worshippers of Chinese *char siu* barbecued pork).

Bearded Clams: A small but growing concentration of shellfish-loving hipsters hailing from Williamsburg, Brooklyn.

Beasties: Advocates of "whole animal" eating, many of whom happen to also be organ-loving OFFALITES.

Bestavores: A term coined by former *New York Times* restaurant critic Mimi Sheraton, BESTAVORES prefer the "best" food products, whatever their geographic provenance. They are in an eternal struggle against LOCAVORES, who forsake foods that are not local.

BILFs: Sexy butchers.

⊸ᴏ

CARNIWHORES (*Homo mediumrareus*)

Characteristics: Though they may not be able to discern apples from oranges, they can distinguish grass-fed from corn-fed beef while blind-folded. Allergic to plant-based foods, these meat-seeking missiles are never happier than when presented with a dry-aged rib-eye steak or a massive lobe of foie gras. To paraphrase the seminal 1980s rapper Sir Mix-A-Lot, CARNIWHORES like pork butts and they do not lie.

Subspecies: Over time, CARNIWHORES have evolved a series of sub-species known as FOIECKERS, OFFALITES, and MARROWVIANS.

Habitats: Large concentrations of CARNIWHORES have been observed at Animal (Los Angeles), St. John Bar and Restaurant (London), Incanto (San Francisco), The Breslin (New York), Checchino dal 1887 (Rome), Cochon (New Orleans), Publican (Chicago), The Meat Hook (Brooklyn), and Au Pied de Cochon (Montreal).

Allergies: CARNIWHORES tend to be allergic to VEGANS; Tofurkey; Meatless Mondays; veggie burgers; and boneless, skinless chicken breasts.

⊸ᴏ

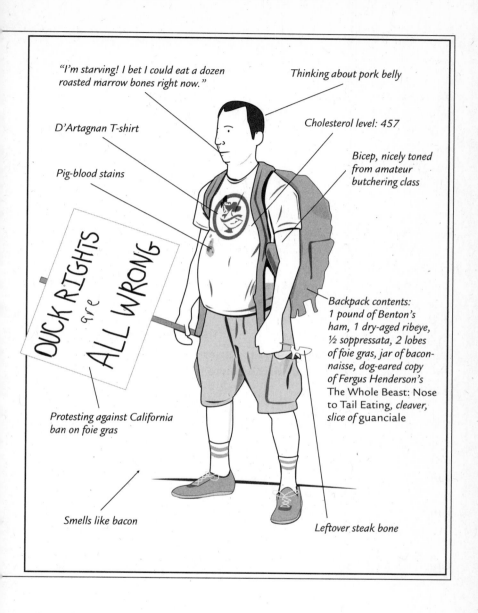

Breisexuals: People who experience an orgasmic response to eating matzo brei.

Burgermeisters: Serious connoisseurs of burgers, they are divided into devotees of high-quality fast-food burgers (in the style of New York's Shake Shack, for example) and those who prefer upscale burgers teeming with foie gras, truffles, and other fancy ingredients. Among the BURGERMEISTERS are the SLIDERATTI, a small subspecies especially interested in miniature "slider"-style burgers.

Candy Freaks: Candy snobs of the highest order, they reject many modern confections in favor of classic candies like the Sky Bar, a milk-chocolate bar containing four sections filled with caramel, vanilla, peanut, and fudge. Their mecca is Economy Candy, the old-school candy emporium located on New York's Lower East Side. A deeply religious order of CANDY FREAKS known as EGGHEADS ritually observes the Easter holiday by savoring and stockpiling Cadbury Creme Eggs.

Carniwhores: A meat-happy race of humans who pleasure themselves with dry-aged rib-eye steaks, blood pudding, pork bellies, and foie gras (see illustration on page 19).

Charcuteristas: While they bear a close kinship to CARNIWHORES for their shared love of meat, CHARCUTERISTAS eschew the cooking of animals over fire in favor of curing them through various culinary schemes involving salts, nitrates, and brines. It is advised to always keep your head down in the home of a CHARCUTERISTA because you may bump into a duck breast hanging from the ceiling as it slowly morphs into duck prosciutto. In Italy, CHARCUTERISTAS are known as SALUMIANS.

Cheftestants: Culinary contestants vying for fame and cash prizes on television reality cooking shows.

Chicken Wranglers: The LOCAVORE movement has spawned a wave of these hardcore local eaters who not only grow their own produce but raise their own chickens, mainly for fresh eggs.

CHILFs: Sexy chefs.

Chocophiles: Chocolate snobs with a deep devotion to all things cacao. A very sensual people, CHOCOPHILES have been observed to have the rare sexual ability to experience chocolate as being orgasmic (see illustration on page 31).

Chowhounds: Dedicated and oftentimes curmudgeonly members of the pioneering online food forum Chowhound.com who tend to obsess endlessly over the latest developments in local ethnic food scenes. A small tribe of disgruntled CHOWHOUNDS left the fold to found the competing online food message board eGullet.

Coffeegeeks: A species of highly caffeinated humans with an unhealthy addiction to coffee, brewing techniques, and coffee-making equipment and gear. They have spawned several subspecies, including the FRENCH PRESSERS, DRIPS, CHEMEXICANS, ESPRESSOVITES, and PERCOLATORI-ANS. Die-hard ESPRESSOVITES are in a constant struggle against the POD PEOPLE, who prefer the ease of using prepackaged ground espresso pods to make their coffee drinks (see illustration on page 23).

Crop Mobbers: A small species of twentysomething hipster foodies who choose to gather at a small farm at a predetermined time to combine their (volunteer) efforts to make intensive agricultural improvements.

Culinary Enthusiasts: A label made up by closeted FOODIES who can't bear to be called by that unspeakable name.

Curd Nerds: Obsessed with curds and whey, CURD NERDS are cheese fanatics whose numbers also include the radicalized LACTIVISTS, champions of raw milk over pasteurized milk (see illustration on page 39).

COFFEEGEEKS (*Homo caffeineus*)

Characteristics: A highly caffeinated species of human with an unhealthy addiction to coffee, brewing techniques, and collecting coffee-making equipment and gear.

Subspecies: This diverse group includes FRENCH PRESSERS, DRIPS, CHEMEXICANS, ESPRESSOVITES, and PERCOLATORIANS.

Habitats: COFFEEGEEKS tend to be highly concentrated in major cities, college towns, and gentrifying urban areas. Large populations are known to congregate in the following cities: Seattle, Washington; Williamsburg, Brooklyn; Portland, Oregon; and San Francisco, California.

Allergies: Cappuccinos after sunset are a sore spot for COFFEEGEEKS, as well as decaf coffee, nondairy creamer, and Frappuccinos.

Thinking about latte art

"Yeah. Last night, I pulled the perfect shot. Twenty-seven seconds. Incredible crema."

Elevated heart rate due to excessive caffeine consumption

Stumptown Coffee T-shirt

Messenger bag stocked with: 2 pounds Stumptown Hair Bender blend coffee beans, Handpresso portable espresso maker, stopwatch (for timing espresso shots), espresso tamper, used espresso-stained copy of William H. Ukers's 800-plus-page 1922 coffee manifesto All About Coffee

To-go coffee, Japanese pour-over style, with grass-fed milk

Forearm, third-degree burn caused by an unfortunate milk-steaming accident

Fixie, a fixed-gear bicycle, the ride of choice for coffeegeeks

On way to a coffee-cupping session

Daily Candies: These upper-middle-class, urban-dwelling, female subscribers to the daily e-mail newsletter "Daily Candy" tend to have a penchant for cosmopolitans, *Sex and the City,* and cupcakes (there are quite a few MAGNOLIANS in their ranks). They are devoted followers of new restaurant openings and have a genetic sexual attraction to the playboy celebrity chef (and total CHILF) Todd English.

Dining Digerati: Recently evolved species of gastronomes who communicate in the form of blog posts, tweets, and message-board postings (see illustration on page 35). A diverse group, they include FOOD BLOGGERS, TWEATERS, YELPERS, GROUPONIES, and CHOWHOUNDS.

Douchebaguettes: The natural mating partner of the AMUSE-DOUCHE, DOUCHEBAGUETTES are easily identified by their fake tans, physical attraction to chef Guy Fieri, and chocolate martinis.

Drunkorexics: Mostly female twentysomething binge drinkers who starve themselves to offset the large numbers of calories they consume in alcoholic beverages.

Femivores: An exclusively female coven of ARTISANALARIANS who combine their interest in food with feminism. FEMIVORES are diametrically opposed to most DAILY CANDIES and DOUCHEBAGUETTES.

FILFs: Sexy farmers.

Finessians: Followers of the überchef Thomas Keller, FINESSIANS use Keller's signature catchphrase "It's all about finesse" as a mantra and treat his *The French Laundry Cookbook* as scripture.

Flexitarians: An umbrella term for fake vegetarians who embrace a mostly plant-based diet yet make the odd exception for animal products like bacon. Their numbers include distinct subspecies such as POLLOTARIANS, who will eat chicken but not meat from mammals, and PESCETARIANS, who eat seafood but not poultry or meat from mammals. Interspecies mating has even produced PESCE-POLLOTARIANS, who consume poultry and fish, but not meat from mammals.

Foieckers: People with an obsessive interest in eating and talking about foie gras.

Food Bloggers: A new and groundbreaking development in the food world is the emergence of this burgeoning species of gastronomes who are pathologically unable to eat, drink, or cook without writing about it on a Web site and posting a photo of their meal. While there are some YELPERS among the ranks of FOOD BLOGGERS, they are generally despised by this group.

Food Jammers: Hipster gastronomes who bring a DIY ethos to culinary challenges such as making one's own Nutella at home, reverse engineering Girl Scout Thin Mints cookies, or roasting coffee using a blow dryer.

Food Nerds: Followers of the television personality and author Alton Brown, FOOD NERDS share a deep interest in food science, though without the cache of MODERNISTS (aka MOLECULAR GASTRONOMISTS).

Foodies: An umbrella term for people with an interest in food, cooking, and restaurants. It has come to acquire an unsavory association with snobbishness or faddishness. As a result, some FOODIES, wincing at the label, self-identify with the unintentionally snobby-sounding name CULINARY ENTHUSIASTS.

Foodiots: A disparaging name for those overzealous FOODIES whose exhibitionistic affection for food, cooking, chefs, and restaurants is an annoyance to his or her peers.

Foodoirists: Memoir writers who can turn any edible experience, from eating a Dorito to their first taste of truffles, into a truth-revealing epiphany.

ॐ

LOCAVORES (*Homo Chezpanissus*)

Characteristics: People who strive to only eat foods that are grown locally. They may live in a house, but they always eat within their "foodshed" (one hundred-mile radius, typically). The LOCAVORE movement has spawned a number of subspecies and splinter groups, including GLOBAVORES, LOCAPOURS, CHICKEN WRANGLERS, and HONEYDRIPPERS, not to mention their natural enemy, BESTAVORES.

Habitats: Berkeley, California, is the mother ship of LOCAVORES, though large concentrations can also be found in San Francisco, Santa Monica, Brooklyn, and Portland.

Allergies: LOCAVORES are known to be particularly allergic to tomatoes after September, out-of-season berries, Chinatown, and bagged salad.

ॐ

Foopies: The foodie equivalent of rock band groupies, FOOPIES blindly follow celebrity chefs, even when they have mostly given up actual restaurant cooking to take up residence in the QVC studios.

Foragers: For FORAGERS, a walk in the woods is like a trip to Costco without the giant tubs of peanut butter. To their highly astute and trained eyes, there might be ramps, mushrooms, wild fennel, mulberries, wood sorrel, and purslane, among other wild ingredients, ripe for the picking. Foragers worship at the soiled feet of the half-man/half–woodland elf René Redzepi, chef of Denmark's famed Noma restaurant.

Freegans: Formerly known as GOBOS (gourmet hobos), FREEGANS are committed to eating food that has been discarded, whether from grocery stores, restaurants, farms, factories, or private homes. Through their actions, FREEGANS seek to expose the immense amount of food that goes wasted while essentially eating garbage for free.

Fruitarians: A subspecies of VEGANS, FRUITARIANS eat a diet that only includes fruits, nuts, and seeds and excludes animal products, vegetables, and grains.

Gastrognomes: Chubby celebrity chefs like Michel Richard and Paul Prudhomme who sport silver hair and beards. Pointy hats are optional (Mr. Prudhomme prefers a white beret).

Gastrosexuals: A corollary to the rise of FOOD DUDES is the emergence of GASTROSEXUALS: men who hone their culinary techniques and use their cooking as a way to impress and seduce prospective sexual partners.

Globavores: Like their brethren the LOCAVORES, GLOBAVORES are committed to local food products and supporting local artisans. However, they are willing to import such products from far-flung places rather than rely strictly upon items sourced from their "foodshed." For example, while a northern Californian LOCAVORE would choose to only consume olive oil produced locally in Napa Valley, GLOBAVORES would gladly buy olive oil made by artisanal producers in Tuscany.

Gluten Freedom Fighters: A fierce group of combatants suffering from celiac disease who are fighting a guerilla war against gluten. Never cross a GLUTEN FREEDOM FIGHTER, but don't eat their pizza, either.

Goodies: Gay FOODIES. Loosely affiliated with TRANS-FATTIES (gluttonous transsexuals).

Grillists: Men who profess to be experts in grilling but claim no other cooking skills (they are especially averse to baking). Most of their numbers are devoted followers of Bobby Flay (from whom they have, in fact, been "licensed to grill") and demigod Steven Raichlen.

Grouponies: Penny-pinching users of Groupon and other daily-deals Web sites. GROUPONIES have a love—hate relationship with restaurateurs, who stomach them for the traffic they provide to their businesses even if they undermine their profit margins.

Gurgitators: Gustatory "athletes" who compete in races to eat large volumes of foodstuffs, from lobsters to asparagus to tiramisu. The Super Bowl of competitive eating is the Nathan's Hot Dog Eating Contest held annually in Coney Island every Independence Day.

Hauties: Snobbish denizens of four-star restaurants.

Hocavores: Sexy LOCAVORES.

Honeydrippers: A subset of extreme LOCAVORES who keep bees, even in urban locales (atop roofs), in order to cultivate their own honey.

Hoppers: A beer-drinking species devoted to tasting, imbibing, and brewing beer. A diverse group, HOPPERS include CRAFTIES (craft beer aficionados), STOUTS, LAGERIANS, PILSNERDS, and ALEWIVES (a small subgroup of female-only beer drinkers with a penchant for herring).

↩

CHOCOPHILES (*Homo cacaous*)

Characteristics: With a bloodstream containing at least 70 percent cacao, CHOCOPHILES are obsessed with all things chocolate (except white chocolate, of course, to which they suffer severe allergies). CHOCOPHILES have the unique sexual ability to experience chocolate as orgasmic. A fair number of chocolate lovers have a strong religious affinity, proclaiming that chocolate is "divine." On the other hand, there are also a significant number of self-hating CHOCOPHILES who believe that chocolate is "sinful."

Habitats: Large concentrations of CHOCOPHILES can be found at: Un Dimanche à Paris (Paris), Jacques Torres Chocolate (New York), La Maison du Chocolat (New York), Recchiuti (San Francisco), and Theo Chocolate (Seattle).

Allergies: CHOCOPHILES are known to be allergic to white chocolate, M&Ms, Hershey Park, and the spelling of cacao as "cocoa."

↩

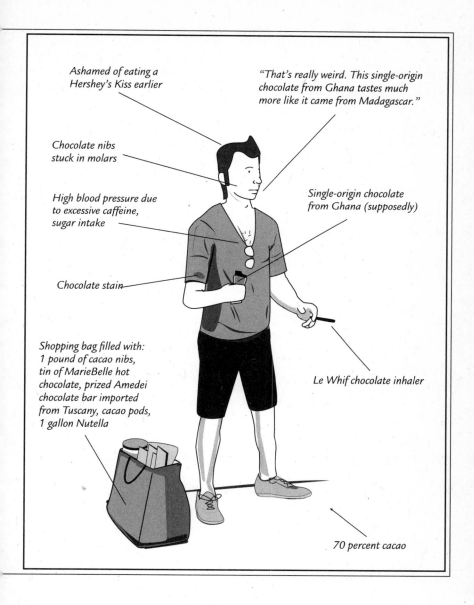

Ashamed of eating a
Hershey's Kiss earlier

"That's really weird. This single-origin
chocolate from Ghana tastes much
more like it came from Madagascar."

Chocolate nibs
stuck in molars

High blood pressure due
to excessive caffeine,
sugar intake

Single-origin chocolate
from Ghana (supposedly)

Chocolate stain

Shopping bag filled with:
1 pound of cacao nibs,
tin of MarieBelle hot
chocolate, prized Amedei
chocolate bar imported
from Tuscany, cacao pods,
1 gallon Nutella

Le Whif chocolate inhaler

70 percent cacao

Lactivists: Antipasteurization activists who champion raw milk for its flavor and nutritional benefits despite laws banning its sale. Many of them participate in underground raw milk co-ops that distribute the contraband milk.

Lardcorists: Chefs and their followers who profess a commitment to "lardcore" cuisine, a term coined by food writer Josh Ozersky to describe "Southern food with hard-core attitude." Their leader is the Charleston-based chef Sean Brock.

Locapours: Individuals who seek to drink only wine, beer, and spirits produced locally. *See also:* LOCAVORES.

Locavores: People who strive to only eat foods that are grown locally—within their "foodshed" (one hundred-mile radius, typically)—whenever possible. It is considered wise to never invite a LOCAVORE to dinner in Chinatown (see illustration on page 27). See also: CHICKEN WRANGLERS, HONEYDRIPPERS, GLOBAVORES, LOCAPOURS, and BESTAVORES.

Magnolians: Extreme cupcake connoisseurs, MAGNOLIANS worship at the temple of all cupcakes, New York's Magnolia Bakery, popularized on the television series *Sex and the City*. The MAGNOLIANS have recently spawned a splinter group, CAKE POPPERS, devotees of bite-sized cakes on sticks.

Manorexics: Men who suffer from eating disorders.

Marrowvians: A subspecies of CARNIWHORES with a serious dedication to consuming roasted bone marrow.

MILFs: Sexy mixologists.

Mister Lattes: Despised by all true COFFEEGEEKS, MISTER LATTES commit the faux pas of drinking lattes and cappuccinos at ungodly hours. They are willfully ignorant of the Italian custom of only consuming such beverages strictly during the morning. Tad Friend, author and writer for *The New Yorker*, is the poster boy for all MISTER LATTES, made famous for his errant coffee-drinking ways in food writer Amanda Hesser's book *Cooking for Mr. Latte*.

Mixologists: Bartenders with a pedigree of combining artisanal ingredients to create new and postmodern classic cocktails. The most pretentious among them call themselves BAR CHEFS.

Modernists: Avant-garde chefs who practice molecular gastronomy yet bristle at the term. Watch out, because if you call them MOLECULAR GASTRONOMISTS they might *sous-vide* you. Better to bite your tongue and refer to them as MODERNISTS.

Mothershuckers: Moms who love oysters.

Noctcarnivores: Food writer and cookbook author Mark Bittman proselytizes this quasi-monkish way of life that combines veganism during breakfast and lunch with carnivorism after the sun sets.

Noodlers: Soup and noodle cultists, NOODLERS are broken down into two major camps: RAMENIACS (lovers of authentic Japanese ramen) and PHOCKERS (devotees of Vietnamese pho soup).

Oenophiles: A cult of wine obsessives, OENOPHILES typically have tannic personalities, teeth stained the color of black fruit, and an oaky finish. They are also frequently drunk off their asses. Included in their ranks are BUBBLEHEADS (sparkling-wine connoisseurs), WHIPPIES (wine hippies who prefer wines made using biodynamic agriculture), STELVINIANS (advocates of screw-cap enclosures on bottles), and CORKIES, who prefer bottles sealed with natural cork.

Offalites: Worshippers of British chef Fergus Henderson and American chef Chris Cosentino, they have a deep fetish for organ meats and other entrails of butchered animals. Though they may have been weaned off the breast by age two, they have been observed to continue to suckle at marrow bones well into their old age.

Olive Gardeners: A lost tribe of Americans who erroneously believe that they have discovered authentic Italian cuisine at the national restaurant chain Olive Garden.

⟨≥⟩

DINING DIGERATI (*Homo internetus*)

Definition: A recent development in the world of food media is the emergence of this large species of gastronomes who chronicle their latest meals in the form of blog posts, tweets, and message-board postings. Though many are quite skilled at using tools (such as cameras) to render appealing portraits of their edible experiences, others should have their camera phones taken away from them.

Habitats: Cyberspace

Subspecies: This growing group has evolved a number of important subspecies, including FOOD BLOGGERS, TWEATERS, YELPERS, GROUPONIES, and CHOWHOUNDERS.

Allergies: This species has exhibited very strong allergies to print food magazines.

⟨≥⟩

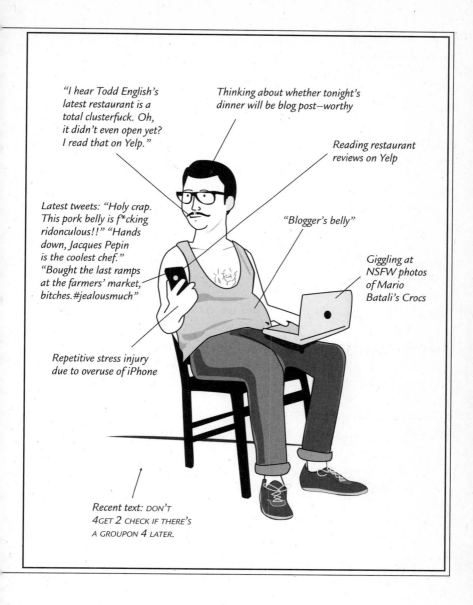

Organistas: A fundamentalist splinter group of ARTISANALARIANS who restrict themselves to purchasing and eating only foods with an "organic" imprimatur. Many ORGANISTAS are also SLOW FOODIES (members of Slow Food, the global food-activist group headquartered in Italy).

Paleoliths: Adherents of the so-called caveman diet, which eschews cereal grains, legumes, dairy, vegetable oils, salt, alcohol, or refined sugars.

Patisserians: Lovers of pastries, their numbers include MACARONAS (addicts of French *macarons*), CAKEHEADS, and the occasional MAGNOLIAN.

Pizzaratti: These pizza snobs are on an eternal quest for pizza perfection and endlessly debate the merits of various types of pizza crust, cheese, sauce, and toppings. The PIZZARATTI suffer from a severe aversion to Hawaiian-style pizza and anything produced by the chain Domino's Pizza.

Rawriors: Members of the raw-food movement, they are the last remaining descendants of those early, prehistoric humans who subsisted on plants before the discovery of fire.

Selmeliers: Students of gourmet salts who have developed an expertise on salt varieties, flavor profiles, and food pairings.

Trader Joes: When nobody is looking, it is not uncommon for some ARTISANALARIANS to sneak out to the chain Trader Joe's for its famously inexpensive processed and frozen foods that are otherwise banned by edict from their demigod Alice Waters. TRADER JOES are in a death struggle against WHOLE FOODIES and are harsh critics of their temple, Whole Foods, which they deride with the derogatory term "Whole Paycheck."

Tweaters: Users of the social media platform Twitter who post 140-character accounts and photos of their latest meals with hyped-up descriptions like "wonderful," "best I ever had," and "ridonculous."

Umami Bombers: Umami addicts who are never without soy sauce, bacon, Parmesan cheese, and fish sauce.

Undercureans: Gastronomes who participate in (sometimes illegal) "underground" eating societies and other alternative culinary gatherings.

Vegans: A lower form of VEGETARIANS, this species only eats plants and eschews all dairy and animal products. To the untrained eye, male VEGANS may look like MANOREXICS. However, despite their gaunt appearance, they are able to maintain an adequate caloric intake by consuming, on average, twenty to thirty pounds of quinoa and kale per day, washed down with five to ten liters of kombucha.

Vegetarians: A peculiar breed of humans that abstains from eating meat, though many will still make an exception for bacon and chicken.

Whole Foodies: Regular customers of the supermarket chain Whole Foods Market.

Yeastheads: Serious fans of artisanal breads, they have forged a tentative truce in recent years with the breakaway rebels known as the GLUTEN FREEDOM FIGHTERS.

Yelpers: Members of the social restaurant review Web site Yelp, which has been criticized (in particular by FOOD BLOGGERS) for the posting of inaccurate information, personal slights, and a general lack of oversight by moderators. Nevertheless, even its most ardent critics will secretly tap Yelp as a resource when searching for a restaurant in an unfamiliar locale.

Zagateers: Somewhat "staid," this group of restaurant-goers "won't go anywhere" without their "little red books," the *Zagat Survey* restaurant guides. ZAGATEERS tend to skew older and find new food media such as Yelp and food blogs to be a "mystery."

❧

CURD NERDS (*Homo camembertus*)

Characteristics: Do you smell something foul emanating from a person nearby? It could be someone with a horrible case of gas, or perhaps a CURD NERD might be lurking with a ripe, room-temperature wheel of Époisses. Curd nerds are devoted to all things curds and whey, the stinkier the better. Their numbers include the radicalized LACTIVISTS, champions of raw over pasteurized milk. An Italian splinter group of CURD NERDS is known as the MOZARELLIANS.

Habitats: Curd Nerds tend to congregate around locations such as Cowgirl Creamery (San Francisco), The Cheese Board (Berkeley), Murray's Cheese (New York), The Cheese Store of Beverly Hills (Los Angeles), Pastoral (Chicago), Artisanal (New York), and Fromagination (Madison, Wisconsin).

Allergies: All CURD NERDS suffer from severe allergies to Velveeta, American cheese (Kraft Singles), and Cheez Whiz.

❧

"I can't believe I'm down to my last raw-milk Camembert. I really need to book a trip to France."

Thinking about sheep's milk ricotta

"My Rind Is Washed" T-shirt

Strong bones due to high calcium intake

Injured finger, accidentally stabbed while cutting the rind off some Stilton

Smells like Époisses

Parmigiano-Reggiano, aged 28 months

Tote bag stocked with: wheel of Humboldt Fog, 2 Burratas, wheel of Cowgirl Creamery Red Hawk, 1 pound of Pouligny-Saint-Pierre goat cheese, slate slab, Laguiole cheese knives, copy of Steven Jenkins's Cheese Primer, baguette

On way to pick up raw milk at secret location

CHAPTER 3

Navigating the Edible Industrial Complex

*Explorations of the contemporary world of food,
including the rise of the celebrity chef,
food trends, understanding restaurant criticism,
and how to communicate with waiters*

"El Bulli Death Trip"

July 2011
ROSES, Spain

In all my years of eating, cooking, writing about, injecting, snorting, and smoking food, nothing could have ever prepared me for the final dinner service at El Bulli, a 269-course meal eaten nonstop over a period of seventy-two hours. This gastronomic marathon alone was daunting, but I had arrived shell-shocked by my unforgettable trip to the restaurant.

I have never been as carsick in my life as I was on that harrowing ride along Spain's Costa Brava to this legendary place. By the way—if you ever wondered—a pound of jamón Ibérico still tastes pretty fucking good even when you are throwing it up, partly digested, from the window of your Smart Car on one of the most death-defying drives known to mankind.

Narrower than a single ass cheek of Calista Flockhart, the road winds endlessly along mammoth cliffs in whose shadows live the ghosts of so many foodies who had died making this terrible journey. One wonders how many lives had been lost on the road to this mecca of molecular gastronomy.

As the car careened—sharks circling in the waters below—the road appeared to be littered with human corpses. Many of the bodies, half-eaten by wild coyotes trained to protect El Bulli from walk-in customers, revealed the telltale signs of culinary travelers. I will never forget one of them, a young man of German origin who must have recently perished. As the wreckage of his BMW burned in flames, he lay on the ground, legs seemingly ripped off, but hands still clutching a Michelin restaurant guide and a bottle of Rioja. He smelled like chorizo.

Another two hundred yards down the road was a small, dusty cemetery. A memorial plaque carved in olive wood that read (in Spanish): "The Foamy Fallen: Here Lie the Heroic Men and Women Who Gave Their Lives to Experience the Cuisine of Ferran Adrià." To be "lucky" enough to nab a reservation at El Bulli and make this horrifying death trip was to face one's mortality head-on and ask the ultimate culinary question: *Will I die tonight just to taste some weird-ass faux olives?* I stopped momentarily to pay my respects to the dead, making some liquid-nitrogen ice cream atop one of the grave sites as an impromptu memorial to these poor lost souls.

THE RISE OF THE CELEBRITY CHEF

One of the most significant events in contemporary gastronomy, aside from the rising interest in organic and sustainable meats and the invention of breastaurants, has been the emergence of the celebrity chef. We won't know for another twenty or thirty years whether the ascent of the celebrity chef was ultimately good for cuisine or even for humanity in general. But for better or for worse, the chef as pop star/entrepreneur/TV personality/bald guy seems to be here to stay.

The Life Cycle of a Chef

Things have changed for the typical career of a chef. Where once a cook might toil away for years in a restaurant kitchen with little chance of upward mobility (much less fame and fortune), today's aspiring chef has myriad entrepreneurial opportunities, from television appearances to selling products, pharmaceutical endorsements, and even starting their own line of shoes. Nevertheless, the vicissitudes of the market make for a great degree of uncertainty. Compare the typical life cycle of a chef then and now.

Age	Then	Now
0	A baby boy is born to humble, working-class parents on the outskirts of a major French capital.	A baby boy is born to middle-class parents in a New Jersey suburb.
2	He witnesses the slaughter of a pig, leaving an indelible food memory and a primal understanding about the relationship between animals and humans.	He witnesses Emeril Lagasse cooking on TV with a studio audience and a live band on the Food Network. Starts yelling "Bam!" at the family dog.
5	Has his first taste of escargots. The earthy taste of the snails, melted butter, and parsley is unforgettable.	Has his first taste of chicken fingers. Discovers they're great dipped in ketchup.
12	Shipped off to work as a *plongeur* (dishwasher) at his uncle's high-end restaurant in Paris.	Shipped off for summer camp in the Poconos.

Age	Then	Now
13	When he's not working twelve-hour days, he spends his limited free time in cafés, where he takes up poetry.	Takes up Nintendo.
15	Advances in his uncle's restaurant kitchen to the position of *garçon de cuisine*, or "kitchen boy."	Advances to the next level of Mario Bros.
18	Works his way up to the position of *tournant*, assisting at various stations throughout the kitchen.	Starts college. Struggles daily to wake up for his first class, which meets at 11:00 a.m.
22	After months of training, he becomes the *legumier*, preparing vegetables and reporting to the *entremetier*.	Graduates college. With limited career options, takes out a $50,000 student loan at an 11 percent interest rate to go to culinary school.
24	When the *potager* (soup cook) suffers severe burns to his hands in a horrible accident involving leek soup, he takes over the position.	Graduates culinary school and takes nine dollars per hour job as a line cook at Olive Garden.
27	Slogs away for fourteen-hour days on the line as a *grillardin* (grill cook).	Depressed and heavily in debt to culinary school, becomes addicted to drugs and alcohol.
28	Develops repetitive stress disorder in his elbow and shoulder from working grill.	Fired from his cooking job, loses apartment, starts living on the streets.
31	Takes over as *garde manger*, the pantry supervisor and chief salad maker.	Talent agent discovers chef, pitches reality TV series called *The Homeless Chef*, which is picked up by a cable television network.
34	Receives his first raise since he was a *plongeur*. Blows it on a new pair of shoes and two packs of cigarettes.	After a successful run on television, picks up endorsement deals from cookware companies and food retailers.

Continued next page

Age	Then	Now
37	Advances to the position of assistant *saucier,* or sauce maker.	Opens a New York City restaurant with seed money from a noted rapper. Wins acclaim for his risottos.
39	Making sauces . . .	Restaurant receives two stars in the *New York Times.*
42	Still making sauces . . .	Expanding his operations, opens up a chain of risotto restaurants, including locations in Los Angeles, Chicago, London, and Dubai.
45	More sauces . . .	Gets own show on QVC hawking exclusive line of silicone risotto stirring spoons.
49	Works his way up to become the vaunted chief *saucier.*	Food poisoning incident at one of his restaurants causes him to eventually fold restaurant chain and go out of business. Loses QVC contract.
50	When the *poissonnier* accidentally stabs himself with a swordfish, he takes over fish station.	Home is foreclosed upon, sells his chef's knife to pawnbroker.
52	Masters deboning a skate.	Ends up back on skid row.
54	Advances to senior role of *chef de partie.*	Discovered in the streets by a cable TV producer, he's invited to return for an appearance on *Homeless Chef: Masters.* Wins competition and gets book deal to write a memoir, which goes on to become a bestseller.
59	Becomes *sous-chef de cuisine,* the deputy chef in charge of the kitchen.	Attends Hollywood premiere of *Rice to Riches,* the movie based on his life.

Age	Then	Now
64	Uncle suffers a career-ending injury slicing potatoes with a mandoline. Takes over as *chef de cuisine*.	Licenses name to a chain of *"risotterias"* with major investment by a shady Serbian private equity firm.
73	Forced to close his uncle's restaurant in the face of competition from a McDonald's that has opened across the street.	Craving risotto, stumbles into his kitchen, but can't remember how to make it.
79	Penniless, he moves in with his eldest daughter.	Honored with Lifetime Achievement Award by the James Beard Foundation.
84	Dies at the stove in an unfortunate, tragic accident while teaching his grandson how to make a classic omelet.	Chokes on a frozen chicken finger while watching an *Iron Chef* rerun and dies a lonely death.

Celebrity Chef Hair

Being a celebrity chef isn't all about culinary technique, ingenuity, or even training and education. One of the more overlooked but essential characteristics in the evolution of the modern celebrity chef is the choice of hairstyle, and, in the case of the male species, choice of facial hair. The selection of hairdo can have far-reaching consequences for one's career. Not only does hair project one's personal style and culinary acumen in a manner that gives an immediate and direct impression of a chef's sensibilities (his or her basic culinary "brand"), in some cases it can also serve a very functional purpose in the kitchen.

1. **The Wet Noodle**
   Chef Mario Batali's taut ponytail not only keeps his hair out of his face while working in a professional kitchen, it also makes for an excellent vehicle for tasting pasta sauces while he cooks.

2. **The Multitasker**
   This vertical, gelled-up 'do favored by *Top Chef* winner Richard Blais is not only a fashion statement, it's an all-in-one natural-fiber scrub and basting brush. A unisex option, a variation on the look, is also sported by chef and Food Network personality Anne Burrell.

3. **The Flavor Saver**
   Chefs Tom Colicchio and Michael Symon are the leading exponents of this classic contemporary celebrity chef look: a smooth, shiny hairless pate (which can be easily wiped clean with a dish towel) paired with a small tuft of hair just beneath the lower lip. The soul patch functions as a sort of "palate palette," containing a miniature *mise-en-place* of flavors, aromas, essential oils, and, of course, the occasional crumb. What's more, the bald head is fantastic for buffing wineglasses and silverware in a pinch.

4. **The Extra-Virgin**
   The secret behind chef Nancy Silverton's renowned pizzas at LA's Mozza? She mops each and every crust with her hair, which has been dipped in the finest Italian extra-virgin olive oil. The oil also gives her curly locks an incredible shine and prevents flyaways.

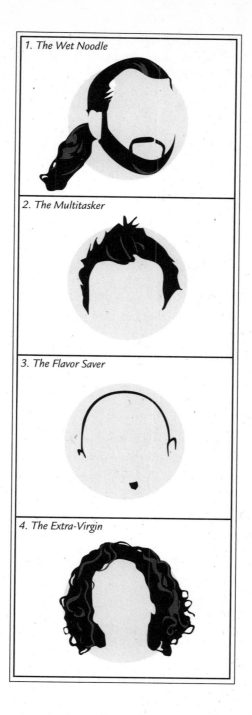

1. The Wet Noodle

2. The Multitasker

3. The Flavor Saver

4. The Extra-Virgin

5. **The Jagger**
Jamie Oliver's "rock star" status is due in no small part to his no-nonsense, mussed-up 'do. The hairstyle evokes the look of late-'60s Mick Jagger, communicating a relaxed confidence, raw sex appeal, and the possibility he just got out of bed with David Bowie.

6. **The Chin Buffet**
A variant of the Flavor Saver, Chef Michael Psilakis combines a bald pate with a full "chin strap" rather than the minimalist soul patch favored by chefs Colicchio and Symon. Like the Flavor Saver, the facial hair can host a wide array of small ingredients, but the greater surface area of Psilakis's Chin Buffet can actually support the weight of small cuts of meat, fish, and fowl.

7. **The Muffler**
Chef Wylie Dufresne is known for his innovative explorations in the field of avant-garde cooking and molecular gastronomy. What people may not know is that his shaggy locks provide a critical layer of protection for his ears when he is experimenting with potentially dangerous materials like liquid nitrogen or using noisy machinery like a centrifuge.

8. **The Finesser**
Chef Thomas Keller's classic hairstyle makes a simple, smooth statement: My lobster is butter poached, and so are my sideburns.

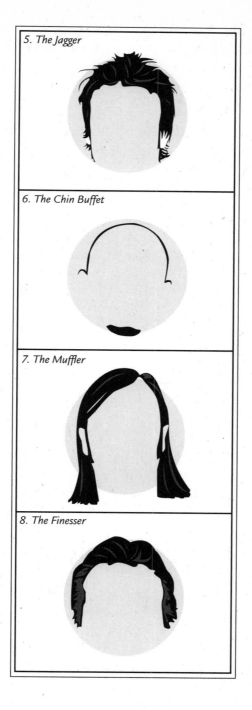

5. The Jagger

6. The Chin Buffet

7. The Muffler

8. The Finesser

A Day in the Life of a Celebrity Chef

Celebrity chefs must juggle an enormous array of responsibilities and commitments. How do they pull it off? Here's an inside look at what a typical day looks like for today's celebrity chefs.

2:00 a.m.
Wakes from a horrifyingly realistic nightmare involving a *lardo*-wrestling match with a nude (but clogged) Mario Batali. Runs to the bathroom and splashes cold water on face, takes two Ambien, and goes back to sleep.

6:15 a.m.
Alarm goes off and he gets up, heads to the kitchen for breakfast. Draws the shades, checks to make sure nobody is looking, and proceeds to eat two Pop-Tarts.

6:45 a.m.
Gastro-yoga session with chef Rick Bayless.

8:30 a.m.
Makes an appearance at farmers' market, meeting and greeting farmers, vendors, and fans. Signs autographs on heirloom tomatoes.

9:00 a.m.
Checks iPhone for e-mail messages, rejects Bobby Flay's friend request on Facebook.

9:30 a.m.
Checks into QVC studio to begin hawking "Press-to-Impress" line of self-cleaning garlic presses.

11:45 a.m.
Sends assistant out for a Big Mac, which is carried back hidden within a Whole Foods reusable shopping bag.

12:30 p.m.
Leaves QVC studio to make rounds at his restaurant, checking on menus, plating, and fondling the hostess in the walk-in refrigerator.

1:00 p.m.
Two-hour nap. Dreams again about the *lardo*-wrestling match with Mario Batali. Heads to see therapist.

3:30 p.m.
Behavioral therapy: Role-play with therapist involves donning orange Crocs, a false ponytail, and rubbing himself all over with *lardo*. He's not sure this is getting him anywhere.

5:00 p.m.
Another round of visits to his restaurant. Takes over the grill station and overcooks three orders of rib-eye steak before the sous-chef diplomatically asks if he can take over. Makes out with the sommelier in the wine cellar.

6:30 p.m.
Dinner with major TV executive to discuss hosting potential new reality show involving celebrity chefs, cooking competitions, makeovers, dancing, and a gross-out *Fear Factor* element.

9:00 p.m.
Walks through the restaurant kitchen and then meets and greets with customers and VIPs. Fondles a busboy in the dessert prep area.

11:00 p.m.
Leaves the restaurant, tickling the dishwashers on the way out.

11:30 p.m.
Weighs himself. Depressed, gets into bed with a box of SnackWell's and falls asleep to a rerun of *Molto Mario* on the Food Network, rekindling his recurring *lardo*-wrestling nightmare.

RUTH'S RULES

The world is your oyster, but only
during months with letter "r."

Endorsement Opportunities: Pharmaceuticals

Celebrity chef Paula Deen's disclosure that she is suffering from diabetes, and her recent multimillion-dollar endorsement of the diabetes drug Victoza present a host of new business opportunities for celebrity chefs. Forget endorsements for pots and pans, Kosher salt, and breakfast cereals; the real money is in pharmaceuticals!

A number of celebrity chefs have smartly gotten on board with this growing area of drug endorsement.

Chef	Drug Endorsement
Todd English	**Aphrodisia,** a prescription medicine that may improve the abs of male chefs.
Bobby Flay	**Grilloft,** a prescription medicine that may relieve pain from burns sustained while grilling.
Rachael Ray	**Yummoza,** an antidepressant that may cause excessive cheeriness in the presence of food.
Eric Ripert	**Frogex,** a prescription medicine that can give native English speakers the ability to talk with a sexy French accent.
Mario Batali	**Crocta,** a prescription medicine that may improve athlete's foot while wearing rubber clogs.
Emeril Lagasse	**Essencia,** a prescription drug that may protect the lungs against accidental inhalation of Emeril Lagasse's Essence spice powder blends.
Guy Fieri	**Reversa,** a prescription drug that may improve rear-view vision while wearing sunglasses on the back of one's head.
Tom Colicchio	**Balda,** a prescription medicine that may help stop the growth of hair on the head while promoting facial hair growth just below the lower lip.
Gordon Ramsay	**Bollox,** an antidepressant that can help with anger management.

Close Encounters of the Celebrity Chef Kind

What happens if you encounter a celebrity chef in the wild (that is, outside of a QVC studio)? Do you immediately run up and give him or her a big hug and a wet kiss? Wink slyly while making a "pack your knives and go" gesture? Throw gang signs? Shout expletives? All of the above?

There is no definitive answer. It will depend upon the celebrity chef and his or her comfort level with public recognition and public displays of affection. For example, while Mario Batali considers it acceptable for fans to remove his Crocs and shave *bottarga* into his mouth, Thomas Keller prefers not to be recognized and to keep it cool.

However, there are some general rules that are advisable for fans to follow when in the presence of any celebrity chef:

» When you see a celebrity chef, please do not ask him or her to talk to someone on your cell phone. Unless, that is, you have chef Ferran Adrià on the line. Celebrity chefs *love* that guy and can talk to him for hours.

» When a celebrity chef is on book tour, make sure to keep all physical contact to a minimum, unless you are bearing foie gras. Then all bets are off.

» If you go to a book signing with Nigella Lawson, try not to fall into her cleavage. You may never get out.

» Bring a first-aid kit to all Paula Deen events. There's a high probability you will be deep-fried.

» Yes, celebrity chefs will sign things besides books. Spoons, cutting boards, mixers, you name it. Most won't sign living things, except for Todd English. He will even sign your private parts.

» Never try to talk to celebrity chefs in a public restroom. That's what private restrooms are for.

» When tackling large book signings, celebrity chefs try to move fast. But they will often ask the hottest men or women to come to the front of the line so that they can get them into bed at a decent hour. This means that less-attractive fans may have to wait a little longer. The chefs appreciate your patience.

» Do: Rub Tom Colicchio's head with the finest extra-virgin olive oil. Don't: Put barrettes in his soul patch.

» If you are lucky enough to hang out with a celebrity chef and smoke some tangerine zest, always pass it on the left.

» If Mario Batali asks you to shave his truffles, you do it.

» When it's over, it's over. Celebrity chefs will gladly stay until the very end of an event or book signing, but then they must leave. In most cases, they need to go and Purell their hands for a few hours after shaking so many of yours.

RUTH'S RULES

Always rub an Iron Chef with a liberal coating
of oil or lard to prevent rusting.

SO YOU WANT TO BE A ... Celebrity Chef

Becoming a celebrity chef is a special combination of raw talent, hair (or lack thereof), genetics, drive, and a pinch of saffron. Do you have what it takes to run a restaurant empire, host a television show, and generally rock out with your crock pot out?

		YES	NO
1	Have you ever made a meal in thirty minutes or less?		
2	Are you bald?		
3	Does the inside of a QVC studio feel homey?		
4	Would you feel comfortable endorsing a line of pet food?		
5	Are you good at coming up with acronyms for everyday food objects (e.g., "EVOO" for Extra Virgin Olive Oil)?		
6	Can you make erotic sounds when you bite into foods?		
7	Do you own a shirt on which flames appear?		
8	When you make pancakes for your kids, do you autograph them?		
9	Do you still wear baby shoes (e.g., Crocs)		
10	Are you willing to take Padma Lakshmi seriously?		

- **If you answered "yes" three times or less:**
  You are clearly not celebrity chef material, but you could always start a food blog.

- **If you answered "yes" four to seven times:**
  Unfortunately, you won't be a celebrity chef, but you are a perfect audience member for ABC's *The Chew*.

- **If you answered "yes" to eight or more questions:**
  You have what it takes to be a celebrity chef! The Food Network will be contacting you shortly.

TREND MAPPING: A FOOD TREND'S JOURNEY

How does an ingredient, a culinary technique, a dish, or a type of restaurant become a food trend? And when does a trend turn from being fresh, novel, and exciting into something bloated, overdone, and, ultimately, despised by tastemakers? Marketing researchers have determined that the journey of a food trend typically passes through eleven basic stages:

» **Stage 1: Discovery**
A guy takes a subway to the wrong station. As he exits, he heads above ground looking for something to eat. The immigrant neighborhood, with its unusual shops and markets and strange smells, baffles, yet intrigues. He goes into a restaurant, sits down, and asks for the specialty of the house—a traditional dish of grilled lamb's kidneys tucked into a puff pastry wrapping, which has gone mostly unnoticed by mainstream America.

» **Stage 2: Broadcast**
The man goes home and posts a message on Chowhound.com about this amazing dish he tasted. Chowhound members are thrilled. Eventually, an argument erupts on the forum over whether or not the restaurant he ate at really serves the most authentic version of the dish. Despite the dispute, interest in the original posting increases and the dish becomes one of the most talked about topics on the Web site.

» **Stage 3: Going Viral**
As chatter on Chowhound grows, the restaurant becomes mobbed with visitors seeking a taste of the dish. Naturally, they report on their experiences eating the dish on Chowhound, Twitter, and blogs.

» **Stage 4: Gastrocolinization**
Hearing about the sensation building around the dish, a well-known chef visits the restaurant and tries it himself. He decides to re-create the dish at his upscale restaurant.

» **Stage 5: Stamp of Authority**
In a restaurant review, the *New York Times* lauds the chef's version of the dish. *Food & Wine* magazine calls it one of the "top 10 new dishes of the year," and *Bon Appétit* deems it "hot."

» **Stage 6: Blowing Up**
The chef launches a spin-off gourmet food truck serving up the dish as a portable, Hot Pockets–style sandwich. Before long, the dish becomes ubiquitous on New York City restaurant menus. Some of the original Chowhounders start to rail against its success and complain about its popularity.

» **Stage 7: Solidification**
The pockets start to appear as appetizers on the menus of national chain restaurants like The Cheesecake Factory, though the basic recipe has been rewritten to use chicken breasts and American cheese. Despite losing its original fan base of die-hard gastronomes, the dish takes off worldwide and is hailed on the front page of *USA Today* as the next big thing.

» **Stage 8: The Foodie's Lament**
The chef shutters his food truck as foodies claim the dish has gone too mainstream. "So over," proclaims the restaurant blog *Eater.com*.

» **Stage 9: Ubiquity**
The food trend reaches its acme as McDonald's starts serving the dish, now recast as bite-size McPoppers. A cookbook devoted exclusively to variations on the dish (original, vegan, Asian fusion), with a foreword by Rachael Ray, is a bestseller. You can even buy a frozen heat-and-serve version at Walmart stores.

» **Stage 10: Backlash**
The food community turns against the dish: The *New Yorker* publishes a ten thousand-word story on the evolution of the food trend, written by Adam Gopnik, including critical quotes from Michael Pollan. The *Huffington Post* includes the trend on its "Food Trends We Wish Would

Die" list, and in a coup de grace, the Berkeley City Council passes an ordinance banning the sale of the original dish and its various permutations within its city limits.

» **Stage 11: Ennui**
Over the next decade, even mainstream America gets bored of McPoppers and the various competitors that have populated the fast-food universe. Demand drops precipitously, and a surplus is donated to foreign-aid groups, from which they are shipped off to feed starving children in Somalia. Finding them inedible, Somalian children use the McPoppers to play checkers and create sculptures that fetch top dollar from tourists looking for local souvenirs.

FOOD TREND FAILS
Some food trends just never take off:

Gluten Lover's Pizza
With the growth of the gluten-free movement and more chain restaurants offering gluten-free options on their menus, some marketing analysts predicted the emergence of a backlash. Pizza Hut responds by launching its short-lived "Gluten Lover's Pizza," which fails miserably.

Nose II Soul
As the so-called nose-to-tail movement became more mainstream, restaurateurs and record companies teamed up to create the failed "Nose II Soul" concept: offal paired with the smooth sounds of '80s R&B group Soul II Soul.

Gourmet School Buses
Nobody could have predicted the success of the gourmet food truck trend, but the idea of combining mobile gourmet food and the movement to improve school lunches turned out to be a dismal failure.

Smart Casual
The success of the "fast casual" chain restaurant, typified by Chipotle, has had plenty of imitators, but perhaps none as unsuccessful as the "smart casual" concept: Banana Republic's failed run at selling tacos.

BREASTAURANTS: BOOM OR BUST?

There has been no stopping the "breastaurant" trend, the emergence of restaurants that draw crowds for waitstaff showing off their, um, "assets." While the megachain Hooters has spawned a number of imitators, other flesh-themed dining establishments haven't experienced the same kind of success.

Below are some concepts for restaurants that tried, but failed, to translate the enormous success of breastaurants into eateries appealing to perverts with other body-part fetishes:

» **Feeteries:** In the late 1990s, a number of restaurants catering to foot fetishists (Toe Jamz, Hogs 'n Heels, and Footburger, to name just a few) emerged, featuring barefoot waiters. A class-action suit filed in 2002 by Toe Jamz staff who reported that they were suffering from chronic athlete's foot destroyed the feetery industry for good.

» **BrASSeries:** Chez Tushé, an informal New York restaurant featuring waiters and waitresses in assless chaps got high praise for serving French comfort food and a large selection of beers, but suffered from Internet chatter about problems with flatulence from the staff. After repeatedly failing municipal restaurant sanitation inspections, Chez Tushé folded. Fattush, a Middle Eastern variation on the BrASSerie theme, never took off, either.

» **Noodle Bars:** Slurpies, a Japanese chain of failed ramen restaurants featuring male waiters wearing only crotchless underwear was successful for two years before being shut down by local health authorities.

» **Thighners:** Gam Grill, a small chain of New Jersey eateries promoted as "the ultimate diner for the leg man" never really took off despite its large portions and large-thighed waitresses. A new owner turned the restaurants into a series of "calveterias" featuring male waiters with well-built calves strutting in high heels, but went bankrupt within just six months.

» **Hipperies:** Fish and Hips, an attempt in Manchester, England, at taking the classic fish-and-chip joint and staffing it with wide-hipped, plus-size waitresses in crop tops and low-rise jeans was an unfortunate failure. Muffin Tops, another failed effort in this vein, was a Seattle muffin bakery featuring staff with bare midriffs and chunky midsections.

HOW TO READ A RESTAURANT REVIEW

Critic Lingo: A Cheat Sheet

Ever wonder what restaurant critics mean when they describe a dish as "toothsome" or praise its "mouthfeel"? Use this handy guide to understanding restaurant reviews and unlocking the secret codes of critics.

Restaurant Critic Term	How It's Used	Meaning
Bustling	The restaurant is known for its **bustling** bar scene.	Make sure to bring earplugs.
Cozy	It's a **cozy** little jewel box of a restaurant.	Be prepared to play footsie with strangers.
Crowd-pleaser	The braised pork belly sliders are always a **crowd-pleaser.**	Tasty, but lowbrow.
Deconstructed	Many of the dishes on the menu are **deconstructed** versions of classic French dishes.	Jacques Derrida would love this joint.
Falls off the bone	The pork ribs, with meat that **falls off the bone,** are phenomenal.	Consult an orthopedist.
Flashes of brilliance	While the menu exhibits **flashes of brilliance,** the entrees are mostly uninspired.	The chef is an enlightened Neanderthal.
Handcrafted	All of the pastas are **handcrafted.**	Made by artisanal robots.

Restaurant Critic Term	How It's Used	Meaning
Hearty	*She specializes in **hearty** fare like short ribs served on a bed of creamy polenta.*	Take two Tums and call me in the morning.
House-made	*Make sure to order the **house-made** salumi.*	Thank God, the *salumi* was not made in the garage.
Molten	*The **molten** chocolate cake, baked to order, is phenomenal.*	Burned the critic's tongue.
Mouthfeel	*The uni has an indescribable **mouthfeel.***	Joker's wild!
Mouth watering	*The flawless menu is **mouth watering.***	Make an appointment to see a specialist.
Offerings	*Among the seasonal **offerings** is a wonderful dish of locally harvested asparagus.*	They ran out of virgins.
Oozes	*The dish **oozes** flavor.*	Apply anti bacterial ointment.
Orgasmic	*The fried chicken was positively **orgasmic.***	Make an appointment to see a gynecologist/urologist.
Plump	*Fresh, **plump** scallops are seared and served atop fresh greens.*	Soft and pliable, like Paula Deen's ass.
Save room for	*Make sure to **save room for** dessert.*	Stop pigging out, you fat slob.
Satisfying	*The roast chicken is deeply **satisfying.***	As pleasing as good foreplay, but short of a climax.
Silky	*The Dover sole is brushed with a **silky** emulsion of lemon, butter, and chives.*	Hugh Hefner would love this dish.
Sinful	*The chocolate gelato is **sinful.***	The critic has religion issues.
To die for	*The basil panna cotta is **to die for.***	Don't drink the Kool-Aid.

Continued next page

Restaurant Critic Term	How It's Used	Meaning
Toothsome	The **toothsome** pasta is cooked perfectly al dente.	Fancy way of saying "chewy."
Updated	The restaurant turns out **updated** Italian standards.	Good luck ordering meatballs here, sucker!
Velvety	The veal is topped with a **velvety** cream sauce.	Tastes like Liberace.

The Dish: The Language of Food

Food is not just food. It's a repository for the food critic's deepest desires, subconscious dreams, secret fears, and eternal longings. The responsibility of the food critic is to tease out those hidden meanings, reflect on past relationships, and explore the very meaning of life. Even if the critic is presented with a simple bowl of macaroni and cheese, never underestimate the opportunity for gastronomic genuflection.

All critics use a simple mnemonic device for creating descriptions of dishes that goes by the easy-to-remember acronym PONTIFICATE. Each letter of the word refers to a specific facet of the dish that must be addressed in the critic's review. Let's take a look at how a critic might use this device to describe a dish of braised short ribs with potato and turnip puree.

P	Peppery	A description of a dish is incomplete without a reference to its essential pepperiness. This is de rigueur for all dish descriptions.
O	Onomatopoeia	Here's where you get to make up words! Can you come up with a word that imitates the sound and feeling of eating the dish? For example, the critic might report that the short ribs arrive "bubbling and burbling" in a cast-iron pot.

N	Narrative point of view	One of the most important decisions for the critic is to choose his or her position in relation to the dish.
		A first-person description might go something like this: *Out of the corner of my eye, I witnessed my waiter bringing me my entrée. Little did I know that I would soon be tasting the short ribs of my dreams.*
		On the other hand, a second-person review speaks directly to the reader: *You are undeserving of this dish. Yes, you may have tasted short ribs, but nothing in your poor little existence could prepare you for the glory of this entrée. You must bow down before it.*
		Another option, though rarely used, is the third-person point of view: *He thought about ordering the roast chicken. But, if he did so, he would have made a horrible mistake. Failing to order the short ribs would represent his ultimate fall into a chasm of despair, which he might never escape.*
T	Transportation	Restaurant critics are frequently "transported" by a dish: *One taste of the short ribs and I was transported to a small village in Provence in the fifteenth century.*
I	Illegality	DO: *The short ribs are so good they should be illegal.* DON'T: *When I went to the bathroom, I peeked in the kitchen and saw that the short ribs were being prepared by illegal immigrants.*
F	Fantasy	The "real" world may not be enough to explain what's on the plate. That's where fantasy comes into play. One critic might merely mention the short ribs' "ethereal" or "otherworldly" qualities, while another may resort to more detailed flights of fantasy: *Were a forest nymph to bed an angel, the wings of its offspring would not be as light as this potato-turnip puree.*
I	Ice-T	A hip-hop reference always enlivens any restaurant review: *I'm a cop killer, better you than me./ Cop killer, fuck police brutality!/ Cop killer, these short ribs are undeniably unctuous.*

C	Childhood	A reference to the critic's childhood is a must: *As I put my lips to my fork, the experience of nourishment and attachment was not unlike an infant suckling at his mother's teat for the very first time.*
A	Avalanches	Ever since the Japanese earthquake of 2011, it has been inappropriate for critics to write about a "tsunami of flavor." Use "avalanche of flavor" instead.
T	Teasing	Many of the world's best restaurant critics were teased as children. As adults, they are still haunted by their youth: *Garlicky and redolent of bacon, the short ribs tease the palate without bullying.*
E	Epiphany	Highlight the revelatory nature of the dish: *I don't consider myself a religious man, but after one taste of these short ribs, I was bestowed with a new understanding of my small place in the universe. If there is a God, he would give this restaurant four stars.*

On the Importance of Being Edited

The contemporary restaurant review is not so much a simple cataloging of a meal but an art form unto itself, where the critic uses the experience of dining in a restaurant for inner exploration, artistic experimentation, name-dropping, and justifying the purchase of *Roget's Thesaurus*. What may be little understood by readers of restaurant reviews, however, is that despite their flights of fancy, by the time a review reaches publication, it has actually been severely edited. Take, for example, this passage from restaurant critic Sam Sifton's October 11, 2011, review of Thomas Keller's Per Se in the *New York Times*:

Per Se's signature starter course is Oysters and Pearls, a dish Mr. Keller developed at French Laundry and brought with him when he moved East. It combines a sabayon of pearl tapioca with Island Creek oysters (small, marble-shaped, from Duxbury, south of Boston, fantastic) and a fat clump of sturgeon caviar from Northern California. These arrive in a bowl of the finest porcelain from Limoges. Paired with a glass of golden sémillon from Elderton, they make a fine argument for the metaphor of transubstantiation.

The appetizer is not food so much as a poem about creaminess, a meditation on brine, a sculpture about the delicious. It is a complete introduction to the restaurant and its pleasures.

As over-the-top as this excerpt may sound, it was nothing compared with Sifton's original draft before it was edited. Courtesy of the *New York Times*—exclusively for publication in this book—here is the original, unabridged version of the passage. Notice how tame the final version is by comparison with Sifton's original draft:

To arrive at Per Se, that pavilion of über-gastronomy in the sky atop the Time Warner Center, is—to borrow a phrase from a great poetess who, alas, has left our shores for London—to feel once again like a virgin, touched for the very first time. The undoing of one's innocence begins with Per Se's signature starter course of Oysters and Pearls, a work of culinary art and extravagance that Mr. Keller developed at French Laundry and brought with him when, in a reversal of Manifest Destiny, he traveled Eastward to open Per Se.

Not only is Oysters and Pearls a sly reference to Prince's "Diamonds and Pearls," it's also a culinary "Rosebud" of sorts for this highly regarded chef, who, in many ways, rivals Orson Welles in terms of the shadow he casts on gastronomy (though his actual shadow happens to be much smaller because he's skinny). The dish is an intermingling—a veritable mélange, if you will—of a sabayon of pearl tapioca with Island Creek oysters. The tiny oysters, round and small, remind one of marbles played with by youths. They undoubtedly call to mind the small marbles a young Tommy Keller must have once played with when he was a small boy, just as Welles's Charles Foster Kane recalls his (spoiler alert) childhood sleigh, Rosebud.

The oysters hail from the wee village of Duxbury, south of Boston, the Massachusetts capital. And, they are to die for, perchance even to drown for given the oceanic environs of an oyster's life, if you'll pardon the pun. They are accompanied by a fat (again, Wellesian) clump of sturgeon caviar from Northern California. The tiny fish eggs also recall Keller's lost youth. Is he even a mammal? Let's not dwell on that in the face of such an awe-inspiring dish. The oysters and tapioca arrive in a round depressed sort of plate one might call a bowl (if they were rubes) made of the finest porcelain, crafted by hand from the tibia bones of baby lions.

When the dish is paired with a glass of golden sémillon from Elderton, one might have a religious epiphany: transubstantiation. For a brief moment, I know not whether it was my imagination, a dream, or something entirely real, the Oysters and Pearls literally became the body of Thomas Keller. God, he was delicious! The chef died for our sins, and since that fateful night, I have taken him as my personal savior. Call me a Kellerian.

Upon further contemplation back home in Brooklyn, that Borough of Kings, I came to the realization that the dish is not food so much as a precocious youngster's novel about creaminess, with Thomas Keller in the role of Harry Potter and Hogwarts being a culinary academy where children practice the unctuous alchemy of gastronomy. It's also a deep meditation on brine that recalls the teachings of the Dalai Lama in his "Policy of Kindness to Bivalves." But no. It is more than that. So multifaceted is this appetizer that to eat it is to feel as if one is standing in a museum of gastronomy viewing a sculpture about the delicious. One may quibble as to whether any human can really comprehend Per Se, but if this restaurant can be known—if it can be understood by our limited brain matter—then Oysters and Pearls is the first step on a journey of enlightenment about Thomas Keller, Per Se, and its many glorious pleasures.

SO YOU WANT TO BE A ... Restaurant Critic

Do you have what it takes to be a restaurant critic? The job requires an enormous appetite, an openness to try new things, a willingness to eat comped meals, and, in some cases, knowledge of how to write (don't worry, that's not always required). In today's changing media environment, it's increasingly difficult to pursue a full-time career as a restaurant critic, so don't worry, you'll still need to keep your day job. Restaurant criticism can be a hobby, like building model airplanes or couponing.

		YES	NO
1	Have you ever uttered the word "mouthfeel" in conversation?		
2	Do you know what salsify is?		
3	As a child, did you tell your mother that her peanut butter and jelly sandwiches were "uninspired"?		
4	Would you accept a free meal in exchange for a review?		
5	Can you use the phrase "redolent of" in a sentence?		
6	Have you ever been "transported" by a meal (across state lines)?		
7	Do you make reservations at restaurants under an assumed name?		
8	Do you have a current prescription for Lipitor?		
9	Did you recently downgrade your mother's turkey from three stars to two stars?		
10	Do you look forward to reading the newspaper on Wednesday mornings?		

● **If you answered "yes" three times or fewer:**
You are not restaurant critic material, but you may be eligible for a membership on Yelp.

● **If you answered "yes" four to seven times:**
You probably won't be able to get a paying job as a restaurant critic, though your friends may pay you to shut up.

● **If you answered "yes" to eight or more questions:**
Congratulations! You have exactly what it takes to be a restaurant critic. Please keep in mind that you also just took a decade off your life expectancy. Enjoy!

DECIPHERING THE MENU

Reading a modern menu can be confusing to even the most sophisticated diner. Here's a simple guide to understanding basic menu terminology:

"Baked": Cooked by a stoner.

"Blackened": The chef is an overt racist.

"Blanched": Tastes like one of the Golden Girls.

"Broasted": Braised and roasted? Boiled and toasted? One of the real enduring mysteries of the food world. Nobody knows what this means.

"Brined": The chef was drunk when he created the dish.

"Butterfly": Very rare gastrosexual position. Also known as a "reverse spatchcock."

"Grill"™: Prepared in the manner of Bobby Flay.

"Planked": The chef lay down on top of the fish and uploaded a photo of said pose to Facebook.

"Smashed": In the case of "garlic-smashed potatoes," this would mean that the potatoes and garlic had hot sex. Otherwise, see BRINED.

"Spatchcock": To split and flatten a whole chicken using only the male genitalia as a kitchen tool. Very sensual.

HOW TO DEAL WITH WAITERS

Dealing with waiters can often be one of the most challenging components of a restaurant meal. Waiters don't do well with typical adult communication. Sometimes they can be as adorable as puppies while other times exhibiting the "acting out" behavior of toddlers. What they need is gentle stroking (literally!). Working closely with child experts and dog trainers, I have identified a series of techniques that can improve your communication with waiters.

» **Make Eye Contact**
Waiters have two things on their minds at all times: tips and cigarette breaks. To get their attention, you need to make strong eye contact. You may even need to verbally address your waiter with a direct phrase like, "Waiter, I need your eyes now."

» **The Approach**
Never approach a waiter directly. Let him or her come to you, and avoid sudden movements that might threaten the waiter.

» **Petting**
Once you have determined that your waiter isn't feeling threatened, gently reach out to pet him or her with your hand just under the chin. Then, you may move on to pet him gently on the side of the face. If you are a regular customer, he may roll over, indicating he wants to be petted on his tummy. Gently rub and scratch the torso (chopsticks may be used in Chinese restaurants).

» **Keep It Simple**
Use short sentences with one-syllable words. Instead of, "Excuse me, I was wondering if you could let me know about your selection of sparkling spring waters when you have a chance?" try something simpler like, "Me want water."

» **Repeat Back to Me**
Sometimes, even "Me want water" is too hard for a waiter to understand. See if he can say it back to you. If not, it may be too complicated.

» **Give Clear Choices**
Clear directions like, "Bring me the appetizer I ordered now or you're going to get a ten percent tip" or "Send my steak back and cook it rare, or suck my ass" are effective ways of communicating what you want while also indicating the consequences of disobeying.

» **Repeat, Repeat, Repeat**
Just like toddlers, waiters have difficulty following directions. You may need to repeat your request multiple times.

» **Rhyme**
"The more you slip, the less I tip." Have your waiter repeat the rhyme.

» **Treats**
Keep a bag of treats at hand. Reward waiters for good behavior and withhold treats for poor behavior.

ETIQUETTE POINTS: THE ART OF EATING WITH OTHERS

Place Setting 101

The basic place setting may appear obvious, but there are multiple ways of approaching your dinner. To paraphrase Gertrude Stein: A fork is a fork is a fork. Not quite.

		Primary Purpose	**Other Uses**
Dinner fork	❶	Forks are primarily used for piercing pieces of meat and vegetables to bring to your mouth to eat. The larger of the two, the dinner fork, is typically used for entrées.	They may also be used to stab the eyes of annoying waiters.
Salad fork	❷	The smaller of the two forks, the salad fork is primarily used for salads and appetizer courses preceding the main course.	Like dinner forks, these also make for great weapons to use against restaurant service staff. The smaller salad fork is well suited to defending yourself against diminutive sommeliers.
Knives	❸	Knives are typically used for cutting larger pieces of meat and vegetables into smaller, bite-size pieces.	You may use the knife as a mirror to detect any attackers from behind you. Moreover, in the event of a surprise attack from the front, you can quickly blind the attacker by reflecting candlelight off the surface of the knife.
Spoons	❹	The spoon is used to lift soups and other liquid or soft foods to one's mouth.	A spoon may be clumsily substituted for a fork or knife (or both) when the diner is very drunk.
Napkins	❺	A napkin is typically placed on the lap and used to wipe away errant food during the meal.	In the event you are served a well-done steak, carefully place the napkin on top of the steak to cover the deceased as a shroud.
Water glass	❻	Use this glass for water during your meal.	For a really good time, fill the water glass to the top with wine.

	Primary Purpose	Other Uses
Wine-glass **7**	Use this glass for wine during your meal.	For a really, really good time, fill the wineglass to the top with whiskey.
Bread plate **8**	The bread plate, set to the left of your place setting, is typically used for bread.	The bread plate may be used to strike the waiter in the event your entrée is delayed.
Nut-cracker **9**	When served lobster, a nut-cracker may be provided for use in cracking the shells.	When served particularly bad food, the nutcracker may be used as a torture device on the testicles of the executive chef.

Eating for Beginners

Now that you understand the basic place setting and how utensils may be used, you may have questions about how to go about eating specific items. If you've ever been presented with a lobster and two spoons, you'll know that it's very difficult to know what exactly you should do in that scenario. Use the guide below to figure out how to handle eating various types of foods.

Food	Technique
Bananas	Though some may prefer to use a pediatrician, it's preferable to hire a mohel. Hold down the banana, wrapped in a talus, and, using a very sharp blade, carefully remove the tip.
Raw vegetables	Some people eat these delicately with their fingers, but it's more fun to throw them at other diners. Have a rubber band on hand to use as a slingshot, especially for radishes and baby carrots.
Olives	Eat the olive with your fingers. If there are pits, aim your mouth at your worst enemy and spit firmly.
Hot dogs	*See above:* Bananas.
Pizza	A slice of pizza should almost always be eaten by hand. In finer restaurants, you might want to consider using a fork and knife. To show off a little cross-cultural flair, try chopsticks.
Bacon	When it is served crisp, bacon should be eaten with the fingers. When it is served greasy and flaccid, it should be flung at the waiter.
Caviar	Except in a casual setting, when you may use your hands, always use a spoon-straw.
Pasta	Twirling pasta on a fork is commonplace. Instead, try braiding your linguine before eating it.
Oysters	Oysters should always be eaten by hand directly from the shells, though the experience is greatly improved if you do use a knife to open the oyster first.

Food	Technique
French onion soup	Traditional French onion soup is covered in a thick layer of cheese. To penetrate down to the soup, it is traditional to use an ice pick or a small jackhammer.
Chicken	Respect the chicken: Hold the breasts with your breasts, the legs with your legs, the thighs with your thighs. If you happen to be a fairy, you can hold the wings with your wings.
Marrow bones	Marrow bones are known as "God's straws" for a very simple reason. They should be brought to the mouth and the marrow should be gently sucked straight from the bones. Should you be sharing marrow bones with your lover, bring the marrow bone between both of your lips and let your tongues intertwine for a very sensual and fatty French kiss.

RUTH'S RULES

After scraping off the edible portion
of an artichoke leaf, use the pointy end to slash
anyone who attempts to eat the heart.

Some Basic Rules of Dining Manners

» **Condiments and Culture**: Always pass the salt and pepper shakers together. It makes a subtle but powerful statement about racial integration and intermarriage.

» **The Art of Chivalry**: When a woman leaves the table, men should stand up. This is an ancient custom that allows the men a better view of the woman's ass as she leaves the table.

» **Elbow Room**: Keep your elbows off the table. That way, you will be better positioned for fighting over the last dumpling, meatball, or other final morsel.

» **Utensil Intimacy**: Kiss a utensil on a first date, but save licking for second dates.

» **Be Sharp**: The best defense is a good offense. Always position the knife so that the sharp side is facing the waitstaff.

» **Be an Architect**: To let your waiter know you are finished with your meal, stack your dishes. It's proper to stack them in a manner appropriate to the cuisine: Build a Leaning Tower of Pisa in an Italian restaurant, a Great Wall of China in a Chinese restaurant, or the Death Star in one of those cheesy sci-fi-themed restaurants.

» **On Grooming**: Grooming yourself at the table, with the exception of shaving your truffles, is never considered to be appropriate.

» **Cell Phones**: Always place your phone on vibrate in a restaurant. Make sure to keep it in your underwear to maximize the pleasure of your meal. If you eat something particularly orgasmic, borrow someone else's phone and give yourself a call. Don't pick up.

Disposing of Awful Food

What do you do when you are at a dinner party and you are given something completely awful and utterly inedible? There are multiple options for extracting the undesirable morsel without making a scene:

» **Go Fish:** Subtly attempt to take the food out of your mouth the same way it went in. For example, if you want to remove from your mouth a piece of chicken that went into your mouth on a fork, you will need to fish around in your mouth with a fork until you can find it and then remove it. This is easiest and least painful when using chopsticks. You may ask a fellow guest to help you, but only ask the person on your left.

» **Swallow:** Close your eyes and swallow the undesirable food. Yes, grin and bear it. Try thinking about chocolate, Thomas Keller in the nude, or fresh strawberries to take your mind off the moment.

» **Spit:** Fake a swallow and gently excuse yourself from the table while the offending bite remains lodged inside your mouth. Depending on the offensiveness of the flavor, spit the nasty bit out in the following areas of the home: in the bathroom toilet (least offensive), on the pillows in the master bedroom pillow (more offensive), in the dollhouse in the child's bedroom (most offensive).

» **Hide and Seek:** If possible, carefully remove the bit from your mouth with your hands and hide it under the garnish. If there is no garnish on the plate, make for a distraction and draw the guests' attention away from the table as you toss it in the salad bowl.

RESTAURANT-SPEAK DECODED

When dining in a restaurant with an open kitchen, you get to be privy to all of the intriguing interactions between the cooks and the waitstaff, which may include yelling, screaming, and lots of ass slapping. This is a great way to learn about how restaurants work and eavesdrop on some fascinating "kitchen talk." But what are they talking about, exactly? Kitchens have a language all their own. Here's a brief glossary of restaurant slang:

Cross-Contamination: Sexual interlude between a waiter and one of the cooks.

Sommelier: Little bitch.

Sanitizing: Spitting in the food before it's served.

Eighty-Six: The kitchen is out of a certain dish.

Sixty-Nine: Two appetizers served side by side and in reverse direction on the same plate.

Haldeman: Host.

Erlichman: Hostess.

In the Weeds: Behind or overwhelmed.

In the Weed: Cooking while high.

Campers: Customers who never leave their table after their meal is complete.

Backpackers: Twentysomething "campers" in Europe.

Comp: To give something away for free. Industry term for serving meals to food writers and bloggers.

Kill It: Cook until well done.

Beat It: Cook until medium.

Tickle It: Cook until rare.

Drop the Check: Take a bathroom break.

Garde-Manger: Salad boy.

Hockey Puck: Well-done hamburger.

Squash Ball: Truffle.

Rollup: Silverware rolled into a napkin. Sometimes smoked by busboys on break.

Sidework: Work performed by the front of the house staff (for example, refilling salt and pepper shakers, polishing silverware and glasses, massage with happy ending).

Waitron: Hermaphrodite server.

Money Shot: Drizzle of crème fraîche.

Walk-In: A refrigerated room for storing the chef's cocaine supply.

Regulars: Fans of a chef who frequent his/her restaurants on a regular basis.

Irregulars: Fans of chef Guy Fieri.

Marry: Method of combining two or more bottles into a single container (e.g., ketchup or jam).

Polygamize: Distribute ketchup from one bottle into two or more containers.

CULINARY TRAVELS: "THAT'S NOT MY RISOTTO" AND OTHER LOCAL FOOD IDIOMS

As you travel the world in search of broadening your gastronomical experiences, you may come across some fascinating food-related idioms. I've collected a few of my favorites from my culinary journeys across the globe.

Drinking

"Snorkeling without a snorkel": *to be a serious drinker* (TAHITI)

"To be like phyllo dough": *to be a lightweight drinker* (GREECE)

"To put a currywurst in your ass": *to get drunk* (GERMANY)

"To take a currywurst out of your ass": *to get really drunk* (GERMANY)

"To wear a croissant": *to throw up* (FRANCE)

"To drop the moussaka": *to throw up* (GREECE)

"To spread one's eyes with crème fraîche": *to have a hangover* (FRANCE)

Cheese, Eggs, and Dairy

"Go fuck an egg": *scramble some eggs* (SPAIN)

"Like *poutine* without the curds": *hopelessness* (CANADA)

"To eat an egg-white omelet": *to marry a cardiologist* (ECUADOR)

"To put skim milk in a cappuccino": *an insult* (ITALY)

"Sunny-side up": *perky breasts* (IRELAND)

"Over-easy": *one-night stand* (BOTSWANA)

"To smell like Époisses": *to be unclean; to need a shower* (FRANCE)

Meat, Poultry, and Fish

"Tastes like chicken": *an insult* (PERU)

"To play with foie gras": *to be jealous* (FRANCE)

"A lamb should graze in your ass": *an insult* (AUSTRALIA)

"To order sausage on the side": *to have an affair* (AUSTRIA)

"To ask the butcher for veggie burgers": *to ask in vain* (RUSSIA)

"Has eaten little prosciutto": *is inexperienced* (ITALY)

"When people ate tuna tartare": *a long time ago* (AMERICA)

"Like a boneless, skinless chicken breast": *pedantic* (PORTUGAL)

"Surf and turf": *bisexuality* (AMERICA)

"Like a vegetarian who eats bacon": *someone without principles* (CHILE)

"To leave the marrow in the bone": *to be foolish* (FRANCE)

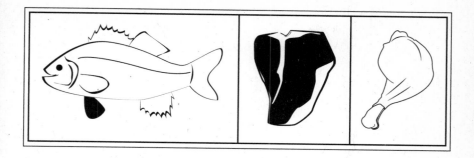

Rice, Grains, and Starches

"Is your penne al dente?": *do I turn you on?* (ITALY)

"Chow fun": *boredom* (CHINA)

"To be like paella without chorizo": *to miss someone* (SPAIN)

"Overcooked linguine": *impotence* (ITALY)

"Pho shizzle": *naturally; of course* (VIETNAM)

"A falafel without tahini": *loneliness* (ISRAEL)

"To be rolled in a tortilla": *to be naïve* (MEXICO)

"To be like a brioche without jam": *to lose one's mind* (FRANCE)

"To eat bread with butter and olive oil": *bisexuality* (ITALY)

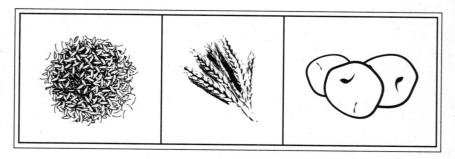

Eating and Dining Out

"Smaller than Sarkozy": *a tiny portion* (FRANCE)

"To be breast-fed by Nigella Lawson": *to eat too much* (ENGLAND)

"To feel like one is eating at Rachael Ray's house":
to eat dull food (LATVIA)

"To go to McDonald's alone": *to feel depressed* (SERBIA)

"Ferran Adrià farted here": *a two-star restaurant* (SPAIN)

"To eat at Denny's with Alice
Waters": *to be delusional* (AMERICA)

"Hungry like Calista Flockhart":
starving (AMERICA)

"Hungry like Paul Prudhomme":
not so hungry (AMERICA)

"To have high ratings on Yelp":
Unreliability (GERMANY)

Fruits and Vegetables

"To shave one's truffles": *to insult one's manhood;*
to emasculate (ITALY)

"Overripe avocados": *blue balls* (MEXICO)

"Little yuzu": *cute girl* (JAPAN)

"A little fingerling": *heavy petting* (PERU)

"To have as many layers as an onion":
to have many sexual partners (DENMARK)

"You're the potato in my borscht":
to be one's soul mate (RUSSIA)

"Putting pineapple on pizza": *an insult* (ITALY)

"To have an asparagus": *to have*
a long penis (NORWAY)

"Go fry some frites": *go fuck yourself* (BELGIUM)

"To be like lumpy hummus":
to feel tired (ISRAEL)

Sweets

"The last spoonful of Nutella": *old age* (ITALY)

"To put salt on baklava": *to spoil a good time* (TURKEY)

"To think one is the chocolate in a chocolate croissant": *to be self-centered* (FRANCE)

"To be more than 70 percent cacao": *to be an honest person* (BELGIUM)

"To be as soft as a flan": *to be out of shape* (CUBA)

"To be rich with Chanukah gelt": *to be not very rich* (ISRAEL)

"To ask for 'Jimmies' on ice cream in Texas": *to be lost or out of place* (AMERICA)

"Like *dos leches* cake": *to be missing something* (PUERTO RICO)

Condiments

"Adding a little *Sriracha*": *embellishing a story* (VIETNAM)

"Pardon me, would you have any Grey Poupon?": *Are you rich?* (AMERICA)

"To put mayo on pastrami": *an insult* (AMERICA)

"Her oil is not extra-virgin": *she is promiscuous* (ITALY)

"To drizzle sesame oil on Cheerios": *to live life to the fullest* (CHINA)

"*Salsa fresca*": *Sexually inexperienced* (MEXICO)

"To whore oneself for balsamic vinegar in Modena": *to be a moral person* (ITALY)

"To rub wasabi in the wound": *self-inflicted pain* (JAPAN)

FOOD CUSTOMS OF THE WORLD: DOS AND DON'TS

When traveling the globe, you will encounter not only many new, sometimes strange delicacies and tastes that you have never experienced, you will also undoubtedly encounter cultures and customs of dining that are very different from what you might experience in the United States. Reading ahead to understand the rules of eating abroad is critical for the culinary traveler. To make things a little easier, follow this cheat sheet of dining dos and don'ts from around the globe.

Japan
DO use your hands, instead of chopsticks, to pick up *nigiri* sushi.
DON'T dip the sushi in ketchup.

Vietnam
DO raise the soup bowl to your mouth to drink the broth.
DON'T pour any of the remaining broth on the chef.

China
DO burp after a meal as a compliment to your hosts.
DON'T fart after the meal as a compliment to your hosts.

France
DO keep your hands above the table during the meal.
DON'T put your hands in your pants until after all the dishes have been cleared.

Germany
DO hold the fork in the left hand and the knife in the right hand and use the knife to push food onto the fork.
DON'T hold the spoon with your toes.

United Kingdom
DO put your fork in your mouth with the tines facing down.
DON'T eat upside down.

Greece
DO smash plates when celebrating.
DON'T smash plates on the busboy's head.

Bangladesh
DO use your right hand for eating.
DON'T use your left hand, unless you are wearing a sequined Michael Jackson-style glove.

Serbia
DO look in the eyes of your companion when toasting a glass of wine.
DON'T try to clink the eyes of a glass-eyed Serbian.

Poland
DON'T sit at the corner of a table if you are an unmarried woman, as it is believed she will not find a husband.
DO sit at the corner of a table if you are an unmarried woman and want to play a casual game of "hide the kielbasa."

Estonia
DO kiss a piece of bread that has been dropped on the ground before throwing it away.
DON'T use tongue, unless it's an artisanal loaf.

Chile
DO use your right hand to pour wine.
DON'T pour the wine into your left hand.

HOW TO SURVIVE A VEGAN APOCALYPSE

As despicable and frightening as their lifestyles may be, there is a very high probability that vegans will outlive carnivores. The lives of vegans might be incredibly depressing, devoid of any real pleasure, and filled with abominable kale farts, but the unfortunate truth is that their plant-eating ways could very well prolong their life spans, leaving a very real threat to the existence of carnivorous civilization as we know it.

The Coming Vegan Apocalypse

Meatless Mondays are just the beginning. Before long, your dreadful week might be defined by Foie Gras-less Fridays, Steakless Saturdays, and even—most hellish of all, perhaps—Soyful Sundays. To prevent the dying-out of carnivores in the face of this veggie burger—eating scourge, you must prepare now for the likely possibility of a vegan apocalypse.

Planning for a vegan apocalypse is not unlike planning for the eventuality of any other natural or man-made disaster. Start your preparation by creating an emergency kit and plan (as detailed below). It's the only way to protect your current way of life and also prevent the rise of a vegan-based society.

RUTH'S RULES

Never look a vegan in the eyes. They will trick you
with their immortality and take your soul.

The "Gastro Bag": Packing Your Emergency Kit

☐ Cured Meats (prosciutto, pancetta, *jamón,* etc.)

☐ Ammunition (Slim Jims, meatballs, and T-Bones)

☐ Charcoal

☐ Livestock (at least two to three pigs or one cow)

☐ Tools and supplies (cleavers, carving knives, cheese knives, tongs)

☐ Hygiene (wet-naps will come in handy for barbecue)

☐ First-aid supplies (Because of their nature, vegans will not bite you, but you should be prepared for the possibility of being smothered with tofu.)

Create an Emergency Plan

1. *Identify the probability of a vegan attack in your geographic area*: Do you live near a Whole Foods? What is the availability of kombucha in your neighborhood? Does a majority of the local population know what "green juice" is?

2. *Choose a meeting place for your family in the event of a vegan apocalypse*: Select a location where you will regroup when vegans have taken over your town. Barbecue joints, butcher shops, and Brazilian *riodizio* restaurants (all-you-can-eat grilled-meat eateries) are all good options. Avoid any cafés that serve soy lattes.

3. *Make a list of emergency contacts*: Police, fire department, cheese shops, propane-gas suppliers, and delicatessens are a must.

4. *Create an evacuation plan*: After initially regrouping with your family, you will need to evacuate to a permanent CSZ (carnivore safe zone) with your loved ones. Research in advance the safest, most direct route to CSZs that have been established in locations such as Memphis, Tennessee, and Buenos Aires, Argentina, among others.

CHAPTER 4

The Gastronomical Me

*How to be a gastronome, including understanding
basic culinary anatomy and how to train your mind, body, and palate
to optimize your gastronomical pleasure points*

"A Zest for Life"

May 1999
NEW YORK, New York

"*Have you ever smoked mozzarella?*" Mario asked, eyes twinkling as he cocked his head to the side.

"*Never,*" I told him. I'd eaten smoked mozzarella, but never made it myself.

"*Well, then, you've got to try it,*" he declared. "*Come in the kitchen.*"

So, I followed Mario over from the dining room to Babbo's kitchen and into the walk-in, where he pulled out a tray full of beautiful white, glistening braids of mozzarella. He grabbed two of them and a paring knife, and I followed him back into the dining room.

"*Now what?*" I asked him, as he pulled out a massive bong.

"*Now we smoke,*" he said.

"*You can't be serious,*" I replied. "*I thought you meant we were going to smoke the mozzarella, not 'smoke the mozzarella.'*"

"*Come on, Ruth,*" he balked. "*You're telling me you've never been gastrostoned?!*"

"*Well, I've never smoked mozzarella.*"

"*Well, then. Let's do this!*"

Mario cut some slices of mozzarella, packed them into the chamber, added some Italian sparkling water, and lit the bong with a flaming branch of rosemary. He inhaled deeply, held his breath, and then passed the bong to me. As he closed his eyes in a lactic stupor, I took a deep hit.

I had never been stoned on mozzarella before, but it was incredible. The flavor was milky, barely tangy, with a hint of rosemary. But, the high was even better. I closed my eyes and had the most vivid culinary hallucination of Jacques Pépin folded inside a giant omelet.

I couldn't believe the sensation. When I opened my eyes, Mario slowly nodded his head, as if to say, "Isn't this the shit?"

It was.

"Now you're ready for the big leagues, my friend," said Mario, as he grabbed a bunch of tangerines and started juggling them. "Hand me that Microplane."

I gave him the Microplane, and he zested the tangerine rind into a small bowl, being careful not to remove any of the white pith. "You don't want the pith," he explained. "Too harsh."

Then, he pulled off one of his trademark orange Crocs and gave it to me. "Take a whiff," he said.

Oh, Jesus, I thought to myself. But I went ahead and raised the clog to my nose. It was a heady, intoxicating blend of cured meats, basil, bottarga, and toe jam. "Hey, give it back!" he yelled. "Don't hog it, dudette! You're worse than Gwyneth."

I handed the clog back to Mario. He buried his nose in it and snorted, then coughed up a chunk of Parmigiano and put the clog down on his lap. "Oops. Sorry about that. Intense stuff!"

He proceeded to pour the zest into the clog, tamp it down with his fat thumbs, and light it with another burning rosemary branch. He showed me how to press my lips up against the holes in the Crocs and inhale. "That's why they have holes," he explained.

At first, everything went dark, and I felt very heavy all of a sudden. Then, the tangerine–zest high washed over me like a giant wave. I closed my eyes and experienced hallucinations of nude chefs chopping giant shallots, pigs (real ones!) in blankets, a baby swaddled in pancetta, and a giant field studded with lobster legs. It was powerful, frightening, gastronomic, and totally fantastic. It was stronger than cocaine and more hallucinogenic than LSD. I was gone. And I was hopelessly hooked.

FOOD 101: INTRODUCTION TO CULINARY ANATOMY

We begin this chapter by exploring the basic anatomy that underlies all gastronomy. When we place a piece of food in the mouth, how does the body digest it? How do we taste it? While the brain plays a key role in how we interpret food, all of our senses, including even the gonads, play a crucial role in tasting everything from the most complex foie gras pâté to a chicken nugget dipped in ketchup. To best understand gastronomy and the power of taste, a basic primer in culinary anatomy is mandatory.

The Mouth: The Gateway to Gastronomy

The mouth is arguably the body's most important orifice. This is not to argue with the importance of the vagina or even the anus, each of which has its distinct benefits, but neither is nearly as effective for consuming food (except, perhaps, *vagina dentata*, but that's for another book). The mouth, in all of its glory, is our primary concern here.

Think of the mouth as the gateway to gastronomy. It's the ultimate starting point on a journey of culinary discovery. The illustration below details all of its most critical parts, from the FORWARD BUMPER to the CRUMB CATCHER, more commonly known by the slang term "lips," not to mention UPPER UMAMI (one of the culinary world's trendiest new neighborhoods).

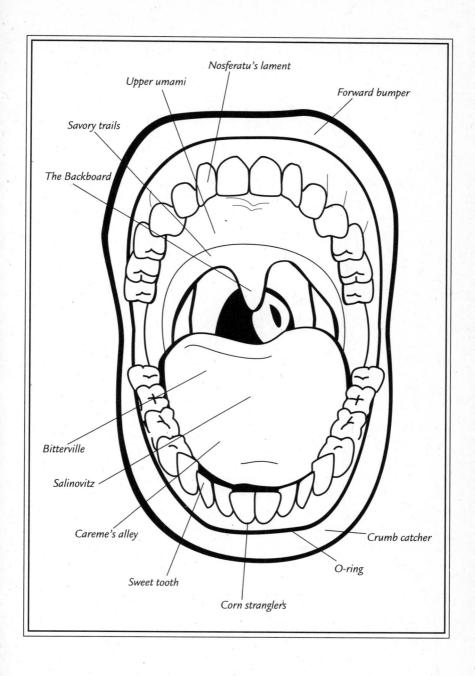

Nosferatu's lament

Upper umami

Forward bumper

Savory trails

The Backboard

Bitterville

Salinovitz

Careme's alley

Sweet tooth

Corn stranglers

O-ring

Crumb catcher

The Body: The Whole Beast

Now let's take a look at the whole beast—nose to tail, if you will. Essentially, the human body is not much more than a fleshy doughnut, with a mess of tissues, organs, and bones surrounding a hole for the entry of food, its digestion, and its final, sometimes painful exit (shell-on shrimp, anyone?).

Also known informally as the "eyes," the OCULARTENSILS help humans to navigate the physical world. But more important, with plenty of practice and expert training, gastronomes can learn the advanced culinary art of "eating with the eyes." Just be very careful with sea urchin and lobsters.

PORTABLE PASTA RACKS, also known as "ears," make for great drying racks for homemade tagliatelle while on the go.

The AROMA SENSOR is designed specifically for smelling foods, enjoying aromas, and detecting who it was that brought a smelly Big Mac into the movie theater.

The mouth, also known as the GATEWAY TO GASTRONOMY, is where it all happens, gastronomically speaking. For a detailed anatomy of this crucial entry point to the body, see "The Mouth: The Gateway to Gastronomy" on page 92.

Also known in some quarters as "chins," the BAR REST evolved specifically for resting the head on top of a bar when sleepy or passed out from intoxication.

The INSULATOR can keep food and drink warm or cold as needed as it descends down the TUNNEL OF LOVE.

The HALF-RACK is a good-size portion of ribs wrapped in a delicious layer of milky white fat. The NIGELLAS similarly contain a portion of ribs and fat, but tend to distract the male's OCULARTENSILS away from their primary gastronomical function.

Also known as nipples, the PALATE CLEANSERS or the AMUSE-BOUCHES may be served as either as a small appetizer or topped with whipped cream for a light dessert.

Here, food departs the TUNNEL OF LOVE and enters the CUISINORGAN, where it is processed by the human body before entering the AMSTERDAM CANAL and VENICE CANAL.

What was once known as food finally departs the body as a warm, stinking mass (not dissimilar from an entree at Applebee's) through the HALL OF SHAME.

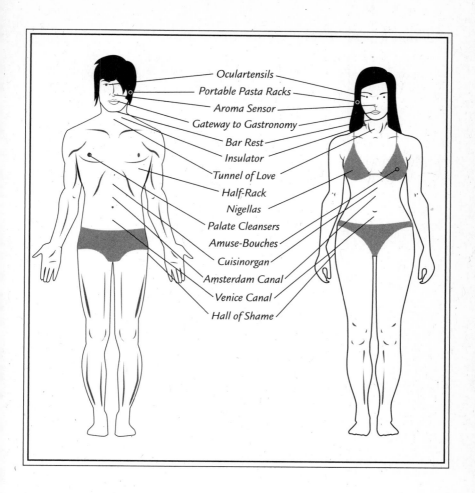

Oculartensils
Portable Pasta Racks
Aroma Sensor
Gateway to Gastronomy
Bar Rest
Insulator
Tunnel of Love
Half-Rack
Nigellas
Palate Cleansers
Amuse-Bouches
Cuisinorgan
Amsterdam Canal
Venice Canal
Hall of Shame

RUTH'S RULES

DO shave your truffles, but DON'T
manscape your peaches.

Evolution: The Rise of *Homo gastronomus*

"Food is culture," it is often said. And yet, in many ways, gastronomy is ultimately biology. Over many, many years, the human body has evolved specific functions that mirror the evolution of cuisine. Modern human beings have become so accustomed to the way the body behaves with respect to gastronomy that many of us have taken for granted how efficiently and effectively it works to promote epicureanism, from eating to cooking and everything in between.

Here are just a few examples of how evolution has served the development of modern (gastronomical) man, scientifically described by anthropologists as *Homo gastronomus*:

» **CANINE TEETH:** Contrary to earlier research, new studies in dental science reveal that these pointed corner teeth evolved specifically to tear open the vacuum-sealed plastic bags used for *sous-vide*.

» **VOMITAL NODES:** Hidden in the spleen, these tiny nodes can detect the presence of Tofurkey and other faux meats and cause a vomit reflex as a physical reaction to ward off ingesting such unsavory foods.

» **BACONOMES:** The act of eating bacon releases these unique hormones that put the body into a state of total euphoria.

» **SRIRACHA SENSORS:** While early man could not stand the heat of spicy foods, modern man developed these peculiar sensors in the lower jaw that actually lower body temperature by as much as 5 percent in the presence of *Sriracha* and other hot sauces.

» **SLURP MUSCLES:** These small yet powerful muscles lining the jaw have evolved specifically to produce the proper level of suction required for slurping noodles from a hot bowl of Japanese ramen.

» **KELLER'S LIGAMENT**: Named after chef Thomas Keller and his in-demand restaurants Per Se and The French Laundry, this crucial ligament in the shoulder makes it possible for the modern human to hold a telephone in the crook of their neck without feeling any pain while spending hours waiting on restaurant reservation phone lines.

» **ROCCO'S CORTEX**: Brain scientists have discovered a small section of the brain that has evolved to suppress feelings of hostility, anger, depression, and utter disbelief over the career trajectory of celebrity chef Rocco DiSpirito.

» **"NUTELLA THINK"**: Just as early man evolved to create and use tools, cultural anthropologists have identified what they term "Nutella think" in modern man: the modern brain's imaginative capacity for identifying things to put Nutella on, from apples to bread to crackers to used cars.

» **CHOPSTICK TENDONS**: Scientists only recently identified these tendons in the hands that play a key role in modern man's unique ability to hold chopsticks, particularly when raising *toro* sashimi from plate to mouth.

» **DRINKY BONES**: Humans evolved a skeletal system (unique among all vertebrates) that provides for excellent balance, support, and stability while consuming large amounts of alcohol while standing up.

» **CACAO ZONES**: Recent studies have discovered these highly sensitive zones on the surface of the body—anatomically similar to erogenous zones—that can lead to chocolate orgasms.

EXERCISING YOUR PALATE: FIVE SIMPLE TECHNIQUES TO BULK UP YOUR TASTE BUDS

Gluttony isn't easy. Like ballet, drawing, or learning the piano, it takes lots of hard work and practice. While there are no shortcuts in the world of food, here are five ways to rapidly ramp up your palate.

1. **The Cleanse:** If you've been eating a lot of processed food, meals at chain restaurants, and recipes created by Food Network personalities, you will need to perform a cleanse of your palate. Over a three-day period, give a shock to your mouth by replacing your toothpaste with a series of edible pastes and mouthwashes:

   Day 1: Brush with anchovy paste, gargle with Meyer lemon juice, and floss with thinly sliced leeks.

   Day 2: Brush with tomato paste, gargle with balsamic vinegar, and floss with angel hair pasta.

   Day 3: Brush with Nutella, gargle with raw milk, and floss with Tahitian vanilla beans.

2. **Weight Training:** Practice using your tongue to lift progressively heavier bite-size pieces of cured meats and aged cheeses into your mouth. Do as many reps as you can until you feel full.

3. **Strengthen Your Core:** Practice this exercise three times per day. While sitting at a table with a (filled) eight-ounce glass in front of you, grab the glass with your right hand and throw your head back until your chin is parallel to the floor and rapidly pour the contents of the glass directly down your throat. Start first with beer, then wine, and then grappa, gradually working your way up to drinks with higher and higher levels of alcohol.

4. **Taste-Bud Aeration:** If you've ever aerated your lawn to promote better grass growth, this technique will be very familiar to you. Stick out your tongue and, using a small fork (a salad fork will do), stab your tongue all over to stimulate taste-bud development. Rub with lime and sprinkle with an organic fertilizer.

5. **Food Porn:** Training your mind is equally as important as training your body. While being careful not to become a food-porn addict, spend at least one hour per day looking at glossy food magazines, food Web sites, and food television. To avoid compromising your palate, avoid the poorly lit, unpalatable photos of dishes appearing on Yelp and some food blogs.

RUTH'S RULES

Always "eat with your eyes,"
but wear protective goggles or you might
scratch your cornea.

SO YOU WANT TO BE A . . . Food Memoirist

Food memoirs (also known as "foodoirs") are big bestsellers these days. Can you turn your personal history into a culinary biography, weaving together relationships and recipes into a seamless narrative?

		YES	NO
1	Was your first taste of foie gras more memorable than your first sexual experience?		
2	Do you own every work by M.F.K. Fisher?		
3	Can you write at least one thousand words about emotional loss and the inside of an Oreo cookie?		
4	Were you abused as a child (e.g., did your parents serve you spaghetti with jarred tomato sauce)?		
5	Do you cry tears made of sea salt?		
6	Can you make an analogy between the death of your grandmother and your first oyster?		
7	Would you describe good onion rings as "revelatory"?		
8	Did you cry when you saw *Julie & Julia*?		
9	Given the choice of writing materials, do you prefer to do all of your writing with squid ink on phyllo dough?		
10	Is chocolate ganache equivalent to sex?		

● **If you answered "yes" three times or fewer:**
You are not quite ready to write a food memoir, but there's always Twitter.

● **If you answered "yes" four to seven times:**
Congratulations, you are qualified to create your own food blog!

● **If you answered "yes" to eight or more questions:**
You have exactly what it takes to be a food memoirist! With any luck, your book could become a feature film and you could sell the rights to your story to a cable television channel.

RUTH'S RULES FOR A HEALTHY DIET

Limit your snacks to unprocessed plant foods.
Next, come up with a new name for "snacks."

...

Breakfast like a king, lunch like a prince,
and dinner like a pauper,
but snack like a marauding Visigoth.

...

Don't eat until you're full. Leave room
to drink until you're bloated.

...

Eat all the junk food you want as long
as Michael Pollan is not looking.

...

Serve a proper portion and don't go back
for seconds. Skip ahead to thirds.

...

Don't eat anything your great-grandmother
wouldn't recognize as food. Unless, of course,
she couldn't see very well.

...

To control portion size, buy smaller plates
and glasses. Then, set the table with at least
two plates and two glasses per person.

...

Eat when you are hungry, not when you
are bored. On the other hand, drinking when
you're bored is perfectly fine. Hic.

CULINARY CODE: A GUIDE TO FOOD ACRONYMS

Whether you are conversing with a friend on instant messenger while searching for recipes online, texting from your smartphone while cooking, or tweeting from your favorite restaurant, you need to know how to communicate quickly and succinctly. In-the-know, technologically-savvy gastronomes use these acronyms to convey key culinary information using the latest technology.

FMLP	Fuck my liver pâté
G2GSR	Got to go stir risotto
IMHO	In my hot oven
FYI	For your ingredient
AP	Asparagus pee
LMAO	Laughing my All-Clad off
NSFW	Not safe for whisking
BRB	Braising ribs in Barolo
RPDOTFL	Rolling pie dough on the floor laughing
FTW	For the wok
WYWH	Wish you weren't haggis
SVMA	*Sous-vide* my ass
TGIF	Thank God it's falafel
STFO	Shut the fucking oven
WWJGVD	What would Jean-Georges Vongerichten do?
AWOL	Absent without lard
BTW	Boneless thighs and wings
BTB	Better than Batali
RAD	Really al dente
SPAM	SPAM

TTYL	Taste the yogurt later
JK	Just kale
NIMBY	Not in my blender, yo!
IM	Incredible mouthfeel
IRL	In restaurant lavatories
SMH	Shaking my hazelnuts
INFL	It's no French Laundry
SOC	So over cupcakes
TLC	Tastes like chicken

CULINARY VESTIGES OF EARLY MAN

Despite evolution's capacity for remaking and refashioning man depending upon natural selection, there remain many curious vestiges of his former self. Scientists have cataloged hundreds of biological oddities in modern humans that can be traced to earlier times in man's history. Most of these body parts no longer play a role in human gastronomy, and yet they are fascinating to explore. Here are just a few:

Flat Molars
These molars, which feature a completely smooth surface, are believed to date back to the 1950s, when man subsisted mainly on soft foods such as tuna casserole, tapioca pudding, and gelatin salads.

Draper's Fold
Named for legendary 1960s advertising man and alcoholic Don Draper, a tiny fold in the liver makes the body and brain otherwise immune to the effects of drinking multiple cocktails at lunch.

Tartare Glands
The science of carbon dating assigns the origin of these unique glands to the early 1980s, when humans subsisted almost entirely on tuna tartare. The glands secrete enzymes that transform tuna tartare into a vitamin-rich superfood.

MIND, BODY, PALATE: GASTRO-YOGA WITH RICK BAYLESS

Chef, restaurateur, author, and TV personality Rick Bayless exemplifies the perfect unification of celebrity chefdom and optimal physical prowess. An avid practitioner of yoga, he is one of the few respected celebrity chefs who is not only recognized as a leading culinary authority on Mexican cuisine, but can also boast an amazingly strong "core" (you should really see his abs).

Rick has kindly shared some of his favorite gastro-yoga positions, which are diagrammed below. Grab a partner and follow these instructions to hone your mind—body—palate connection:

1. **The Taco**

   Lie on the floor on your back, side to side with a partner. Both partners should carefully push up with their outside arms and bend their outside legs at the knees to form a unified, cupped shape akin to a taco. Add filling of choice (e.g., roast pork, chicken, or steak), along with chopped onions, cilantro, and a squeeze of lime. Breathe and hold for four to six breaths.

2. **The Huitlacoche**

   While your partner stands erect, arms raised high to mimic a corn cob, grab him around the neck with both arms and pull yourself up, knees up tight to your chest, to mimic *huitlacoche* (fungus) forming on a corn husk. Breathe and hold for two to four breaths.

3. **The Burrito**

   Spread out a blanket on the floor. Lie on top of your partner, face-to-face. Add beans, rice, and shredded cheese. Grabbing one corner of the blanket, roll until you are completely enveloped by the blanket. Hold the position for four to six breaths.

4. The Quesadilla

Three people are required to complete this advanced yoga pose. Draw straws to determine who will be the "cheese" (the other two will be the "tortillas"). The first partner should lie down on the ground, faceup, arms and legs spread wide. The second partner should lie down on top of him, facedown, arms and legs spread wide. The third partner should lie facedown on top of the "cheese," legs and arms spread wide. Salsa and guacamole are optional. Hold the position for two to four breaths.

THE JOY OF COOKING: A CULINARY KAMA SUTRA

Writer Michael Ruhlman, the noted author of *The Making of a Chef* and *Ratio* and coauthor of *The French Laundry Cookbook*, is widely regarded as one of the food world's leading exponents of food porn. He has written particularly eloquently about the art and pleasure of lovemaking while cooking:

In my prekid days, I lived with my wife in a shaded little bungalow in Palm Beach, Fla. The evenings were balmy, and I thought nothing of getting dinner rolling, then coaxing my wife into a little preprandial fling. What better way could there have been to pass the time while the charcoal turned to burger-searing embers? There was no better appetizer, and the meal afterward was remarkably satisfying.

Ruhlman is such a gastrosensualist that he even created a recipe for roast chicken that explicitly calls for having sex with your spouse after you've put it in the oven (no pun intended). "Cooking—and having sex for fun—is what makes us human," writes Ruhlman. "To deny ourselves either diminishes the creatures that we are, and to practice both with greater frequency and competency deepens our humanity, which leads to a more fulfilling life. All good things. Roast chicken and sex: They're good for you!"

Ruhlman should be applauded for his thoughtful consideration of the possibilities for sex while cooking, but roast chicken is really just the "tip" of the iceberg (pun intended). Why limit your gastrosex life to just one dish when there are myriad opportunities to get yourself off while cooking? Once you start thinking about it, there's a shocking amount of downtime in the kitchen that can be exploited for sexual gratification. But before you get too excited, do note that it's not going to be possible to incorporate sex into every recipe. For example, don't even try anything sexual while making risotto; there's simply too much stirring involved.

Clip and save this handy chart (laminating is highly recommended) for some basic rules to follow to get more sex into your life while cooking:

While Cooking...	...Perform This Sex Act
While roasting a chicken...	...have intercourse with your spouse.*
While roasting a turkey...	...have intercourse with five to ten spouses, depending on the size of the bird.
While toasting a bagel...	...rub up against the counter.
While steaming rice...	...pleasure yourself.
While slicing melons...	...think about Nigella Lawson's cleavage.
While steeping hot tea...	...get teabagged.
While steeping iced tea...	...teabag somebody.
While braising short ribs...	...have a three-way.
While boiling water for pasta...	...get a blow job.
While boiling the pasta...	...give a blow job.
While making an omelet...	...peek at nude photos of Jacques Pépin.
While grinding coffee...	...goose somebody.
While grinding spices...	...get goosed.
While warming a corn tortilla...	...imagine caressing Bobby Flay's hot pepper.

Always thoroughly clean your hands with soap and warm water to avoid cross-contamination.

RUTH'S RULES

Treat meat as a flavoring. For other meats.

Sexy Food Talk: Some Culinary Pickup Lines

Let's face it: Restaurants, food shops, and markets present tremendous opportunities for the mingling of the sexes. While you're at the butcher checking out rib eyes, a lovely young lady or a handsome young man may catch your eye. Attraction can be elusive, but if you're prepared with an appropriate pickup line, you might just find your match. Try these epicurean lines, which pair beautifully with their gastronomic environs.

Cheese Shop	"Are you into *affinage*? Because I'd really like to check out your cheese cave."
Butcher shop	"Hey, you look like you're in serious need of some tube steak."
Japanese Market	"Is that your friend over there? *Shiso* fine."
Delicatessen	"This pastrami is hot. And so are you."
Middle Eastern Restaurant	"Try the *fattoush*. It's amazing. Well, almost as amazing as yours."
Foraging Expedition	"If you really want to get wild, I've got some ramps and morels back at my apartment."
Bagel Shop	"I'm not into everything bagels. I only want you."
Supermarket	"Get outta my dreams. Get into my cart."*
Pastry Shop	"The way you pronounce *macaron* is so wrong, I don't want to be right."
Cupcake Shop	"I have to tell you, you have a fantastic body, even if you have a buttercream face."
Sushi Bar	"Miso horny."
Chocolate Shop	"Wow. This chocolate is orgasmic. And so am I."
Coffee Shop	"Normally, I buy whole-bean coffee, but I'd rather grind with you."
Bar	"I like my martinis stirred, not shaken. Just like my clitoris."
Ramen Shop	"Do you mind if I slurp your noodle?"

Apologies to R&B singer Billy Ocean.

Fast-Food Chain	"Guess what? That's not the only thing that's super-sized right now."
Chinese Restaurant	"I noticed you ordered the General Tso's Chicken, because I have a Major Hard-On for you."
Indian Restaurant	"Oh, don't eat that. It's not *raita*. I just can't control myself around you."
Spanish Restaurant	"You should take your shirt off. I'm pretty sure this is a 'topless' restaurant, not a tapas restaurant."
French Restaurant	"I noticed you ordered the foie gras terrine in aspic. I think we could really gel together."
Ice Cream Shop	"Nice scoops."
Vegan Restaurant	"Soy vey, your ass is tremendous."
Bakery	"I can't decide between the *ficelle* or the baguette. How big do you like it?"
Farmers Market	"You've got some really nice melons. Are they heirloom?"
Italian Restaurant	"I like my women like I like my olive oil: extra-virgin."
Frozen-Yogurt Shop	"May I taste your Pinkberry?"
Vietnamese Restaurant	"I don't know what's hotter, you or this *Sriracha*."
Pizzeria	"Make that a large with pepperoni delivered to . . . your apartment."
Wine Shop	"Are you into Stelvin closures? Because I totally want to screw you."
Fish-monger	"Is that a geoduck clam in your pocket or are you happy to see me?"
Cookware Shop	"Hey, I noticed you were looking at the crock pots. Think of me as a human slow cooker. I can go for *hours*, baby."
Tea Shop	"I usually drink loose tea, but I'm always down for some teabagging."
Fried-Chicken Joint	"Those breasts look delicious. And the chicken doesn't look bad, either."

Beyond Aphrodisiacs: Getting Freaky with Food

There is a great deal of literature devoted to the aphrodisiac potential of various foods, but the actual evidence that any food can actually have an effect on sexual interactions between two persons is quite limited and mostly unconvincing. To date, the only detailed study of the relationship between food and sex revealed a causal link between bananas and intercourse. Apparently, there are many documented cases of nude couples accidentally slipping on banana peels and falling into various coital positions. However, those are really just accidents, not proof of a food's intrinsic properties as an aphrodisiac.

But what about sex *with* food? This may be uncharted territory for some, but there are actually plenty of fruits, vegetables, seafood, and meats ripe for your sexual gratification. And we're not talking just the usual carrots, cucumbers, parsnips, and overripe melons. Here are a few of the most sensual foods you may not have had the pleasure of experiencing:

1. **Coco de Mer:** Also known as the Kim Kardashian of the plant world, this massive seed of the fruit of the Coco de Mer palm tree, native to the Seychelles, happens to be shaped like large, protruding woman's buttocks.

2. **Geoduck Clam:** The "Long Dong Silver" of bivalves, the geoduck clam is famed for its unique appearance and texture and is a notable ingredient in Asian cuisine. Its long, trunklike body can protrude twelve inches or more from the shell. A word of advice if you are to attempt sex with a geoduck clam: A visit to a urologist first to obtain a prescription for Viagra is highly recommended.

3. **Asparagus**: Asparagus was considered to be such a phallic symbol that it was banned from girls' schools in the nineteenth century. And, for good reason: It's long, lovely, and naturally ribbed for her pleasure. If you are married or in a relationship, be very careful of your liaisons with this vegetable, because your spouse or partner may detect the telltale smell of asparagus in your urine.

4. **Liver**: Is there a more erotic piece of prose than Nobel Prize–winning author Philip Roth's description of an interlude between a young boy and his family's dinner in his novel *Portnoy's Complaint?* A soft, slippery engorged liver, filled with blood, is the perfect erotic companion on a lonely night in a butcher shop.

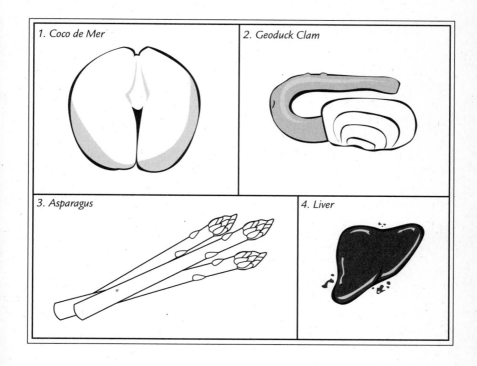

1. Coco de Mer

2. Geoduck Clam

3. Asparagus

4. Liver

THE ART OF GETTING GASTROSTONED

Controlled substances and cooking go together like pasta and Parmigiano-Reggiano (especially when you use a piece of ziti to snort some freshly grated cheese off the back of your Italian dealer, but I'm getting ahead of myself). Nevertheless, pairing drugs and food can be a dangerous game. The risks of bringing drugs into the kitchen can potentially be lethal. After all, how many pastry chefs have gone up in flame caramelizing crème brûlées while high on crack cut with Muscovado sugar?

Drugs have a long and storied history of being an important source of inspiration to the culinary artistry of many professional chefs. Dubbed "haute stoner cuisine" by *New York Times* reporter Kim Severson, this is food that is not only born from the mind-altered state of a totally wasted chef, but equally appeals to anyone with a palate and a case of marijuana-induced munchies.

But before you jump headlong into the wonderful world of combining illicit drugs and gastronomy, bear in mind that there is a right and a wrong way to proceed. Consider these basic rules for the beginning gastrostoner:

1. DO use cocaine to increase your speed when beating egg whites to stiff peaks.

2. DON'T freebase near a grass grill.

3. While waiting for bread to rise, inject yourself with horse tranquilizer.

4. Choose your drug and food pairings wisely. For example, pair Thai sticks with pad thai, hashish with corned-beef hash, and opiates with poppy-seed bagels.

5. To avoid cross-contamination, store your herb separately from your herbs.

6. When serving cocaine at a formal dinner, always place the coke spoon to the outside of the soupspoon.

7. When serving meats paired with methamphetamines, cut the meat into bite-size portions and be sure to remove all knives from the table.

8. When stoned, always shop the middle aisles of the supermarket to find highly processed snack foods that are high in salt, fat, and HFCS.

9. Drink the bong water.

....

GASTROSEX INTERNATIONAL: FOODGASMS AROUND THE WORLD

Once you have begun to explore your culinary sexuality, there's no stopping. Broaden your horizons and travel to these locales to sample their unique gastrosexual traditions. You won't be disappointed.

Regional
Barbecuekakke (Memphis)
Hot Doggy—Style (New York)
Deep Dishing (Chicago)
Mission-Style Burrito Position (San Francisco)

International
Quesadillingus (Mexico)
Phollatio (Vietnam)
Bulgogasm (South Korea)
Foieplay (France)
Amuse-Tush (Belgium)
Teabagging (United Kingdom)

ON PARENTING: RAISING A GASTRONOME

Adult gastronomy and all that it entails (the orgies of pork belly, tangerine-zest hangovers, and espresso highs) is strongly rooted in a rigorous epicurean upbringing. Forget chicken fingers, because when it comes to kids' appetites, they actually have a natural, untapped hunger for escargots, foie gras, and *lardo*. Your job, as a parent, is to tune out the marketing messages of the commercial food industry and encourage your child's innate cravings for the good stuff.

Infants

The introduction of the first solid foods is a crucial stage in your baby's gastronomic development. During the first six months of life outside of the womb, a baby's needs can be met entirely by breast milk. However, after the age of six months, the baby may begin to show signs that she is ready for solid foods. These behaviors may or may not include:

» Wanting to put things in her mouth.
» Interest in foods eaten by others.
» Subscriptions to food magazines.
» Starting a food blog.
» Ability to suck small amounts of marrow from a roasted bone.

When the baby has exhibited some or all of these telltale signs, you can begin to introduce solid foods. It's wise to gradually introduce new foods, one at a time, in the following order:

1. **Cookies:** The baby has solely been drinking milk for six months. That's a very long time to just drink milk without any access to cookies. Start by introducing chocolate-chip cookies, a natural with breast milk, before working your way up to more sophisticated shortbreads. At this young age, when the baby's motor skills are still developing, avoid biscotti or any other cookies that require dunking.

2. **Pâtés:** Soft purees like liver pâté are a great way to encourage early development of the baby's palate. Start with chopped liver from your local Jewish deli before working your way up to pâté de foie gras.

3. **Cereals:** Cereals are very common first foods for a baby, especially when getting high with a newborn. Start with a crowd pleaser like Cap'n Crunch or Cocoa Puffs. At all costs, you must avoid rice cereal, which tastes like warmed-over wet cardboard.

4. **Fruits and vegetables:** Optional.

Toddlers

Toddlers are notoriously picky eaters. However, recent research suggests that their disdain for anything "green" on their plate could be a natural defense against veganism (a reaction that should be strongly encouraged by parents). Here are five strategies to improve toddlers' eating habits and encourage their young palates:

1. **Family Meals:** Family meals are a soul-destroying ritual that should be abandoned by parents. Kids who take part in regular family meals endure horrendous arguments, painfully bland conversations, and incredibly mediocre food. Instead, encourage toddlers to dine out on their own. Epicurean parenting means setting up your toddler with her own credit card and teaching her how to make a reservation at trendy restaurants. While she's at it, she'll also learn some important life skills like how to use the phone and maintain her own calendar.

2. **Variety:** Serve a variety of foods. Too many kids subsist on plain old macaroni and cheese. At the very least, change up the usual by adding some shaved truffles, or, better yet, rich nuggets of lobster meat.

3. **Be a Role Model:** Teach your children by being a good example to them. Be aware of how your behavior can profoundly influence your child:
   » Never drink light beer or wine coolers in front of a child. It will scar them for life.
   » Always order your steak rare.
   » Eat a proper portion size (as a general rule, a 3:1 ratio to the portion Michael Pollan would eat).

4. **Avoid Battles:** Don't fight battles with your children over food. Sometimes, you have to simply go all out and declare war. As a disciplinary measure, you may ultimately be forced to resort to the nuclear option: serving them Tofutti instead of real ice cream.

5. **Get Kids Involved:** Get your children involved in the kitchen. No child is too young to start washing dishes or sharpening knives. By age three, it's perfectly appropriate to teach them how to butcher a whole animal. Start with a chicken and work your way up to a whole hog.

Teens

The teenage years are a time of major change. As teens enter adolescence, they begin to make more of their own food choices. However, as teenagers become young adults, parents can still play an important role in guiding their culinary development:

1. **Calcium Intake:** Calcium is critical to bone development, particularly for teenage girls, so it's important to make sure that teens get an adequate amount of calcium in their diets. It's also a great way to forestall any experimentation with veganism. Keep your kid hooked on milk, yogurt, and cheese so that they don't give up dairy products, at least while they're living under your roof. There's not much you can do once they leave for college, where veganism can be rampant.

2. **Increase the Iron:** Girls, in particular, need more iron during their teen years. Consider this your "license to grill": adolescent girls should eat at least two to three steaks per day, preferably washed down with a cow's blood smoothie.

3. **Talk to Your Teen:** Your teen's body is going through many changes. Your child may begin to explore his or her sexuality. They may have questions for you like, "Can you get pregnant from eating whale sperm?" Or they may begin to have fears like, "I think I might have spotted dick. What do I do?" Talk to them about the changes they are experiencing and empower them with information and knowledge. This way, they'll feel prepared when they have their first experience with chocolate that is orgasmic.

RUTH'S RULES

Remove skin and excess fats from meats
before serving them to your children.
Then eat them when they're not looking.

A BASIC GUIDE TO PORTION SIZE

How do you know that you're eating a reasonable amount of food? Bull testicles come in pairs, so that's an obvious portion size. But it's not always so easy to know how much is appropriate to eat when it comes to other foods. If you really want to watch your diet (if you're into weird stuff like that), it's important to get a handle on portion size. Use the following guide to help visualize appropriate sizes for the foods you eat.

1. **Nuts**
   A small handful is a good portion size for nuts, so long as elephant testicles aren't on the menu.

2. **Fish**
   A proper portion of fish is about the size of a checkbook. Use one of those Publishers Clearing House checks as a standard measure.

3. **Meat**
   The palm of the hand is a good rule of thumb for a correct portion size for meat, provided you use Hulk hands as a baseline.

4. **Ice Cream**
   A half-cup of ice cream equals the size of a lightbulb. A good portion size is the number of bulbs it takes to illuminate a night game at Yankee Stadium.

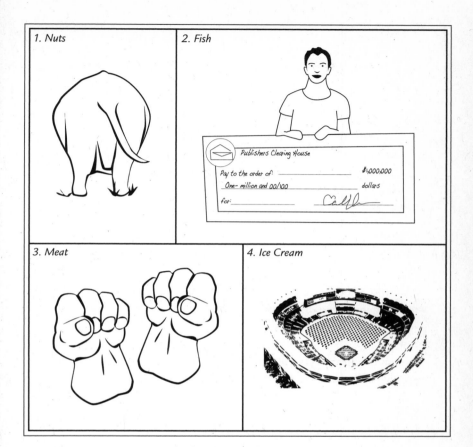

5. **Butter**

   One teaspoon of butter is about the size of a Scrabble tile. Limit your portions to words like "supercalifragilisticexpialidocious." Go for a triple-word score to increase your portion size.

6. **Cake**

   One slice of cake is about the size of a deck of cards. But remember, Jokers are wild. Draw one and you can eat the whole damn cake.

7. **Cheese**

   One ounce of cheese is about the size of four dice. Roll four sixes and you can eat an entire wheel of triple crème Brillat-Savarin.

8. **Chocolate**

   If one ounce of chocolate equals one package of dental floss, eat the amount of chocolate equivalent to the number of packs of floss it would take to clean the teeth of a *Tyrannosaurus rex*.

9. **Pancake**

   If a single pancake is about the size of a DVD, a proper portion size is equal to the number of DVDs you will find in the boxed set of the complete collection of James Bond films.

5. Butter

SUPERCALIFRAGILI—
STICEXPIALIDOCIOUS

6. Cake

7. Cheese

8. Chocolate

9. Pancake

007

ME, MYPLATE, AND I

In June 2011, the United States Department of Agriculture (USDA) secretary Tom Vilsack, First Lady Michelle Obama, and Surgeon General Dr. Regina Benjamin joined together to unveil the USDA's new food infographic, MyPlate. It replaced the iconic food pyramid and its towering heights of oils, fats, meats, and cheeses atop a broad base of bread and pasta (doesn't that sound incredibly delicious?). Although MyPlate received little news media coverage, when the USDA cast out the food pyramid, it also did away with the Egyptian theme altogether, getting rid of its lesser-known Drinks Sphinx detailing recommendations on the daily recommended intake of libations.

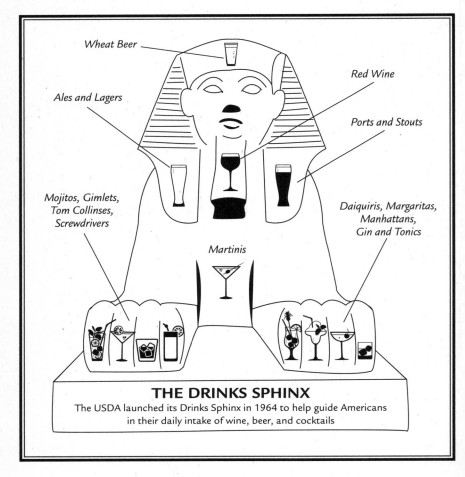

Wheat Beer

Red Wine

Ales and Lagers

Ports and Stouts

Mojitos, Gimlets, Tom Collinses, Screwdrivers

Daiquiris, Margaritas, Manhattans, Gin and Tonics

Martinis

THE DRINKS SPHINX
The USDA launched its Drinks Sphinx in 1964 to help guide Americans in their daily intake of wine, beer, and cocktails

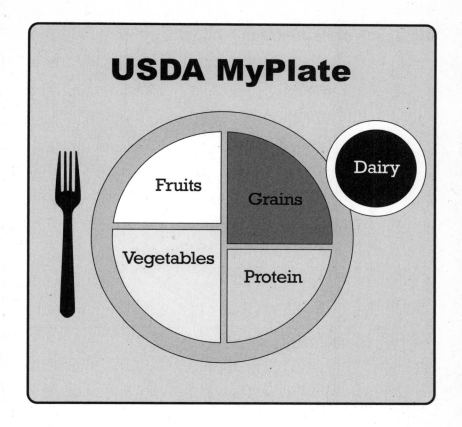

The aim of the pyramid's replacement was to encourage food choices that increase the intake of grains and greens. According to Secretary Vilsack, "MyPlate can help prioritize food choices by reminding us to make half of our plate fruits and vegetables and shows us the other important food groups for a well-balanced meal: whole grains, lean proteins, and low-fat dairy."

But does a one-size-fits-all MyPlate really fit the needs and fetishes of our diverse and pluralist gastocracy? Americans pride themselves on individual freedom, liberty, and the right to supersize things. Here are some alternative MyPlates that better reflect the diets of our diverse nation of gastronomes.

The Carnivore's MyPlate

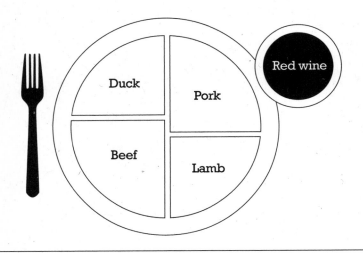

The Vegan MyPlate

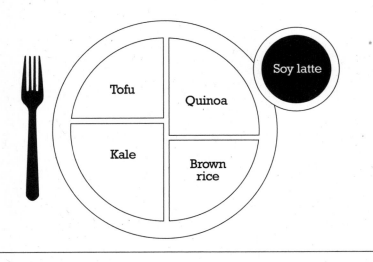

The Alice Waters MyPlate

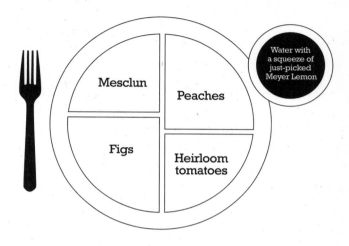

The Noodle Lover's MyPlate

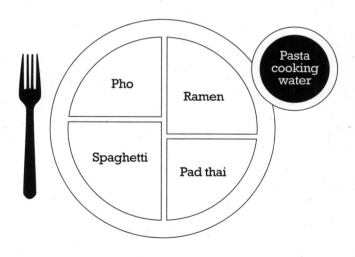

The David Chang MyPlate

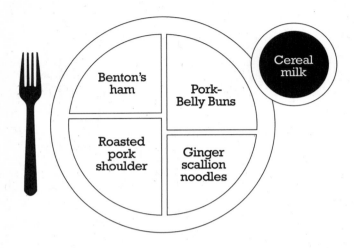

The Paula Deen MyPlate

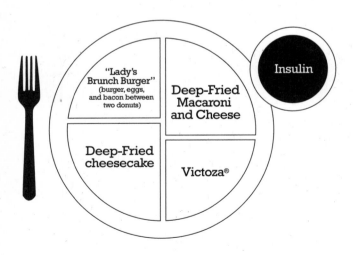

CHAPTER 5

Matters of Taste

*Lessons in food and flavor, from cheese
to chocolate, herbs, and meat*

"Down and Out in London"

April 2003
LONDON, England

I'll never forget the time I ate oysters in London with Gordon Ramsay. It started out great. A night in a fantastic hotel with just me, Gordon, and five dozen bivalves on a king-size bed of crushed ice. It was beautiful, or so I thought.

"Fetch me a little of that mignonette, love?" Gordon purred as he lounged on the bed, naked.

I was so stoned on tangerine zest that I went and put a teaspoonful right on top of his "bangers and mash." Gordon grabbed my arm by the wrist and shouted at me.

"Bollocks! Not there, you fucking nitwit! Jesus fuuuuucking Christ, what the fuck is wrong with you, you fucking idiot?!"

It was insulting—and he was extremely obnoxious—but the swearing also kind of turned me on. I could see why he was so successful on TV. Brazenly, I went and squeezed some lemon on him, too.

"Fuck this! Are you fucking kidding me?!" he shot back.

He jumped up from the bed and toweled off. "What the fuck do you think you are fucking doing?! The mignonette goes on the fucking oysters, not on me! The lemon is supposed to be squeezed over the fucking oysters! Oh, fuck it all!"

"OK, OK, Gordon. Why don't you just smoke some zest and chill the fuck out."

"You know what? You have a serious fucking problem. You're a fucking zest addict." And he was right. After all these years, maybe I had smoked too much. Gordon put on a robe and went to the door, where he whispered to someone on the other side.

"Who's there?" I asked.

"Just some friends."

It sounded like a chorus.

And then, into the hotel room walked some of the world's top chefs and food personalities: Tom Colicchio, Mario Batali, Thomas Keller, Joël Robuchon, Pierre Hermé, Jacques Pépin, Alice Waters (hate her!), Wolfgang Puck, and Bobby Flay.

"We're here for you, Ruth," they said in unison.

"What the fuck are you talking about?" I asked.

"This is an intervention," said Thomas Keller. "Listen. You've been smoking way too much tangerine zest. You're really starting to lose your perspective. Look, Gordon just told me you tried to put mignonette on his, um, manhood. Now, you know that's just a waste of good mignonette, Ruth." Gordon nodded in agreement.

"You need to get off the zest and get back into cuisine," said Tom Colicchio, who proceeded to take my Microplane zester from the nightstand and bend it with his bare hands until it was in the shape of the letter u and completely unusable.

"Nooooooooooooooo!" I cried, shrieking.

But maybe they were right, I thought to myself. Smoking a little zest was OK, but maybe I had gone too far. I was losing my sense of reality, trading in the taste of real flavors, real culinary experiences, and real food for a cheap citrus high. Maybe putting mignonette on Gordon Ramsay was my way of hitting rock bottom.

Soon I found myself in a group hug with some of the most celebrated chefs in the world. They helped me renew my interest in gastronomy. They brought me back from the edge.

In Chapter 4, we explored the basics of culinary anatomy and methods for honing your mind, body, and palate for optimum gastronomical enjoyment. Now it's time to put this knowledge to use when it comes to matters of taste. In this chapter, we'll investigate coffee, meat, cheese, herbs, pasta, and chocolate. Along the way, we'll also touch on food safety and the steps you can take to protect yourself from the risk of food-borne illness.

CUP THIS: HOW TO TASTE COFFEE

Do you love a decaffeinated hazelnut-flavored coffee from Dunkin' Donuts with plenty of sugar and skim milk? If so, please skip ahead to the next section. We're here to talk about tasting actual coffee, not sweetened brown milk.

Tasting coffee is a complex interaction that involves all of the tongue's most basic senses (sweet, sour, salty, and bitter) as well as the all-important sense of smell. The process of tasting might appear simple (it's more than gulping and gargling), but it's actually extraordinarily complex, and can be broken down into three major steps:

1. **Fragrance:** The first step in the tasting process is to discern the coffee's fragrance, a step that occurs before brewing even begins. As you grind the coffee, ask yourself what your first impressions are of the fragrance. Get up close to the grounds. Really close. Use a coke spoon to snort some up your nose, or a razor blade to create a narrow line for snorting.

2. **Aroma:** Next, when you have actually started the brewing process and water makes contact with the coffee grounds, aroma is released. Get as close as you can to the freshly brewed coffee without severely burning your nostrils. Some blistering on the surface of the nose is perfectly fine (have bandages on hand). Coffee connoisseurs develop tough calluses ("coffee callous"), which over time become extraordinarily resilient to heat.

3. **The Nose:** The final step is to take a sip of the coffee. Counterintuitively, this is known as "the nose." As you advance in your coffee tasting, you can try more advanced tasting methods such as "the ear," "the toe," and the most advanced of all, "the mouth."

The Elements of Taste

Once you have taken a sip of coffee, look for three major elements: body, acidity, and balance:

Body is the textural sensation of drinking coffee. Is it "oily" like a used car salesman or former Republican presidential contender Herman Cain? Is it lightweight like Michele Bachmann? Perhaps it feels thick in your mouth and makes you want to gag, like oral sex with John Holmes.

Acidity refers to acids in the coffee beans that combine with natural sugars during the brewing process and provide a sharp, tangy flavor. You'll notice high levels of acidity if the coffee is redolent of throwing up after a night of drinking an entire bottle of Kahlua.

Balance is the way that all the elements of a coffee harmonize. In this way, a coffee with very good balance should resemble Boyz II Men in their prime.

Coffee Characteristics

Just as wine connoisseurs have a complex language for analyzing the flavors in wines, so, too do, coffee snobs have an entire lexicon for describing a cup of joe:

Bright: This coffee could totally get into Harvard.

Caramelly: Like a Twix bar, but without the cookies or chocolate.

Carbony: Burnt, charcoal overtones reminiscent of that time you found yourself chewing on briquettes while drunk.

Earthy: Tastes like dirt. Delicious dirt.

Fruity: Having an aroma similar to berries, citrus, or Nathan Lane.

Grassy: Duuuuuuuuude . . .

Mellow: This coffee is perfectly happy sitting back and listening to some Steely Dan.

Musty: Smells and tastes like your grandma's linen closet.

Nutty: An aftertaste similar to testicles.

Spicy: Having a flavor redolent of Spanish actress/guitarist Charo.

Spunky: Reminiscent of Punky Brewster.

Wildness: A gamey flavor. A particularly "wild" coffee is known in coffee-tasting circles as "buck wild."

Winey: A coffee with all the qualities of a good red wine, except for the alcohol (dammit).

What Your Coffee Brewing Style Says about You

Coffee Brewing Style	Coffee Snob Rank	Method	What It Says about You
Drip	1	One of the most common forms of making coffee: Coffee grounds are placed in a paper or metal basket in a drip coffee machine and water passes slowly through the grounds, filtered by the basket, into a glass or thermal carafe.	You lead a depressingly drab suburban existence. You read *USA Today* and revel in the coupon pages. Though you once used to drink French-press coffee in your twenties following a semester abroad at the Sorbonne, in your middle age you now prefer the ease, indeterminate flavors, and complacency of drip coffee.
Moka	2	Sometimes referred to as a "stovetop espresso maker," this Italian coffeemaker uses steam pressure to draw water from the bottom chamber of a Moka pot through coffee grounds and up into a second chamber in the top, where the coffee is emptied.	An Italophile, you drive a Fiat 500 to work and go for bike rides on a mint green Bianchi. In your spare time, you read short stories by Italo Calvino and weigh the comparative pleasures of penne versus rigatoni.
French press	3	Coffee is brewed by infusing coffee grounds in hot water in a special pot equipped with a plunger that is depressed to separate the grounds from the coffee.	You have a vague memory of being raised by a French nanny. As an adult, you daydream of living in Paris. You read the *New York Times* and revel in the Sunday paper's crossword page. You like to wear corduroy blazers with arm patches and think actress Juliette Binoche is pretty hot.

Coffee Brewing Style	Coffee Snob Rank	Method	What It Says about You
"Pour over"	4	A minimalist Japanese brewing method that at first glance might look like the drip method, but uses specially designed tools to brew by the cup. No coffee machine is used. Water is poured a few ounces at a time from a special kettle with a very narrow spout in a circular motion over coffee grounds placed in a paper filter inside a special, grooved coffee dripper.	You treat making a cup of coffee like a tea ritual. A Japanophile at heart, you have a serious devotion to Japanese design, eat sushi, and harbor a secret fetish for Hello Kitty. You are in a committed relationship with a body pillow imprinted with a life-size image of a Japanese anime character. Nothing's better than snuggling up with the pillow and a freshly brewed cup of pour-over coffee to watch an Akira Kurosawa DVD.
Espresso	5	Using an espresso machine, hot water is passed through packed, finely ground coffee via steam pressure.	You are a coffeegeek of the highest order. You live for perfect crema, get angry when you can't get a decent *ristretto,* and look down on people who don't own burr grinders. You have considered appearing on the cable television series *Hoarders* due to your humongous collection of demitasse cups.

CUTTING THE CHEESE

Every cheese tells a story. A slice of processed American cheese is a sad tale of misspent youth as remembered by a palate-less man imprisoned in a jail made of orange plastic. On the other hand, a wheel of Époisses is a biographical account of a lonely Frenchman who, shunned by his friends for his awful body odor, can never share his true secret: His heart is made of buttercream.

To discover a cheese's story and experience its being in all of its many facets—flavor, texture, color, and stankiness—you need get up close and personal with your cheese. That doesn't mean you need to sleep with your cheesemonger, though it does help (the least you can do is offer to wash his rind). However, once you purchase your cheese and take it home, unwrap it and observe its many variables:

» **Color:** The color of cheese can vary greatly, so it's useful to be as accurate as possible as you assess its hue. Take a look at the rind. Is it rusty? If the answer is yes, get specific. Is it rusty like 1974 Pinto hubcaps or Redbeard's pubes? Is it white and chalky? Then "Cullen clan" might be a fairly good descriptor. On the other hand, "dirty homeless socks" is the most typical way of describing the Spanish goat's milk cheese Garroxta.

» **Firmness:** Hard, firm cheeses are generally described as "Team Jacob." The softest cheeses are sometimes called "Bataliesque" or "Kirstie Alleyish." On the other hand, a "tight" cheese might be described as "Nigella's sweater."

» **Flavor:** How do you describe the flavor of the cheese? Is it goaty or "Sarah Jessica Parkerish" (horsey)? Perhaps it's "Bootsy" (funky) or "James Francoesque" (herbal)?

» **Aroma:** Is there a noticeable aroma? Would you say it's barnyard? Be more precise: chicken shit, cow pie, goose doody, or farmer's diarrhea? Or maybe you find it musty? Which is the better descriptor: week-old underwear or Vegas prostitute?

Some Guidelines for Serving Cheese

» **Cut the cheese fresh.** This can be a delicate balancing act. While cheese should always be cut fresh, you may not want to cut the cheese directly in front of your guests, particularly your mother-in-law. In the case of particularly stinky cheeses, most cheesemongers will recommend you cut the cheese in the bathroom and spray the cheese with Febreze before returning to the table to serve your guests.

» **Temperature.** Always serve cheese at room temperature. The colder the cheese, the less flavor. If the cheese gets too warm, you can give it an aspirin. Use a rectal thermometer for the most accurate temperature readings.

» **Use the right tools.** When it comes to knives, I like to plunge a sharp dagger deep into a wheel of Parmigiano-Reggiano; the first one who can pull it out gets the title of King of Cheese. For melting cheeses, I recommend eating them with a spoon—straw. For oozing cheeses, it's always a good idea to keep some antibacterial ointment and bandages on hand.

» **Smoked cheeses.** Smoked cheese is not for everybody, and you run the risk of becoming a cheeseaholic. But it's a great way to share an evening with friends. Mozzarella and Gouda are the most popular cheeses for smoking. The easiest way to smoke cheese is to wrap a piece in parchment, light one end, and inhale the other. You may also try using a bong, which is better known as "fondueing." Instead of water, fill the bong with dry white wine and a little Kirsch and only use a high-quality Gruyère or Emmenthaler (or both). Be prepared for some really weird hallucinations involving the Swiss Family Robinson.

ALL ABOUT MEAT

The Basics of Buying Meat

When it comes to buying meat, labels can be very confusing. Visit any supermarket meat section and you'll discover a plethora of labels that are intended to provide more information to consumers so that they can make more informed choices. But with so much information to sift through, all of this labeling can often do more harm than good.

Here's an easy cheat sheet to basic meat labeling:

» **Natural:** Does not contain artificial colors, flavors, chemical preservatives, or silicone breast implants.

» **Grass fed:** Cattle and lamb that exclusively smoked marijuana.

» **Organic:** Meats with a USDA ORGANIC label must not be raised with growth hormones, they must eat organic feed, they must not be administered antibiotics, and they must have access to open pastures and Alice Waters's cell phone number.

» **Free range:** This label, which applies only to poultry, means the bird has access to the outdoors at least five minutes a day, where they may enjoy cigarettes and lift weights with other prisoners.

A Guide to Meat Grades

Federal-government inspectors grade beef according to an eight-point scale that assigns a series of labels based on quality:

1. **Prime:** The highest-quality meat. Prime meat comes from younger cattle and is known for its marbling.

2. **Choice:** Choice meat has less marbling and is less tender than prime but can still taste good.

3. **Select:** Usually leaner and less flavorful than prime or choice meats. Can be cut into thin strips to wear as suspenders.

4. **Utility:** You can find this meat in dress-shoe soles, hot dogs, or at your favorite chain restaurant.

5. **Hobo:** This grade of meat is typically enjoyed on boxcars.

6. **Pet worthy:** Dogs may be willing to eat this grade of meat, but not cats.

7. **Hobby:** Inedible by humans or any mammals, but great for arts-and-crafts projects.

CHECKING FOR DONENESS: THE FINGER TEST

There's a very simple test you can use to tell if your meat is done using just a touch of your finger. Press on the thickest part of the steak with your index finger and determine how well done the meat is based on the following guide:

Rare: The steak is rare when the meat is as soft as Paul Prudhomme's ass.

Medium: The steak is considered medium when it has the texture of Giada De Laurentiis's cleavage: soft but springy and bouncy to the touch.

Well Done: The meat is well done when it is very firm and there is absolutely no give when touched, like Todd English's abs.

Treat meat as a special-occasion food.
For example, only eat meat on days that begin
with consonants.

Offal Good: Twenty Organs to Eat Before You Die

Offal, or organ meats, have become increasingly popular ingredients in contemporary gastronomy. Once considered peasant foods, these "nasty bits" have gone mainstream, prized by some of the world's most celebrated chefs, not to mention the television series *Fear Factor*. But please don't stop at pork bellies, beef cheeks, and marrow bones. There's a whole world of nasty bits out there for your gastronomical exploration.

1. **Blood vessels:** Serve them just as you would pasta. Capillaries make a great substitute for angel hair, while larger arteries can replace *bucatini* in your favorite pasta dish.

2. **Salivary glands:** Mouthwateringly delicious sautéed with olive oil, garlic, and sea salt.

3. **Esophagus:** Stuff these with your favorite sausage.

4. **Gallbladder:** An acquired taste, gallbladders can be quite bitter due to bile. However, if you like broccoli rabe, you may well enjoy this organ. Be careful of gallstones, however.

5. **Pancreas:** Not only can you eat the pancreas, you can squeeze out the pancreatic juices over ice for a summer refresher.

6. **Rectum:** Treat these as you would a chile relleno, stuffed with cheese and rice.

7. **Anus:** Deep-fry them by the basketful and serve with aioli as you would fried calamari.

8. **Hypothalamus:** These secrete some really cool hormones like dopamine. Smoke them using a trachea (see below).

9. **Bladder:** Serve filled with lemonade.

10. **Urethra:** These don't taste all that good, but they make for great straws.

11. **Tonsils:** These can be hard to find unless you live near a children's hospital. Serve them with ice cream.

12. **Adenoids:** See *Tonsils*.

13. **Hangnails:** Grind in a mortar and pestle with olive oil, pine nuts, and cheese for a wonderful pesto (garlic is optional).

14. **Spinal cords:** Serve them in soup and slurp them like noodles.

15. **Ovaries:** Known as the "caviar of the land," scoop out the eggs with a mother-of-pearl spoon and serve with toast and crème fraîche.

16. **Nipples:** Roast and salt them as you would nuts.

17. **Prostate:** Classic finger food.

18. **Trachea:** They don't call this the windpipe for nothing. Use it to smoke a hypothalamus (see above).

19. **Ligaments and tendons:** Talk about toothsome; these can be a little chewy. They make great substitutes for chewing gum.

20. **Larynx:** Not only is the larynx also known as the voice box, delicious braised, roasted, or steamed, it's also a great conversation starter at parties. Literally.

BASIC FOOD LABELS

Enriched: Nutrients were lost during processing, so the product was adulterated with gold by a leprechaun.

Fat Free: Inedible "foods" that are made to resemble real foods but contain less than .5 grams of fat per serving. Some fat-free products, like fat-free yogurt, may be used as substitutes for household items like spackle.

Healthy: Marketing term for "tastes bad." Avoid these.

Low Sodium: This helpful label, which denotes that a product contains 140 milligrams of sodium or less per serving, lets you know when to grab the saltshaker.

Natural: Free of Botox, silicone implants, or other plastic surgery.

Sugar Free: At least 54 percent wood by volume.

HERBS FOR SEASONING AND FOR SMOKING

In cooking, herbs and spices can be used to add flavor to a dish, infuse a stock, or, when they are introduced at the very end of the cooking process, add a powerful element of aroma to the finished product. But herbs and spices are also known for their mind-altering properties. To appreciate their hidden potential, you must unearth their hallucinogenic powers.

There is, perhaps, no writer more eloquent on the subject of getting high on herbs than Sir Thomas More, who wrote: "As for rosemary, I let it run all over my garden walls, not only because my bees love it but because it is the herb sacred to remembrance and to friendship, whence a sprig of it hath a dumb language." Dumb language indeed: One of the well-known side effects of smoking rosemary is slowed speech.

What's more, anyone who has ever listened to Simon and Garfunkel's ode to herbal euphoria, "Scarborough Fair," knows these guys got seriously high on parsley, sage, rosemary, and thyme. But why stop there? There's a whole world of herbs and spices waiting for your experimentation:

Type of Herb or Spice	How to Use	Typical Hallucinations
Anise	Smoke	Being whipped with black licorice sticks by a giant stalk of fennel.
Basil	Make a paste with olive oil and pine nuts and take orally.	Vivid dreams of cavorting on the beach with Mario Batali in Liguria, Italy.
Cayenne pepper	Snort	Body on fire; Emeril Lagasse tickling you and repeatedly yelling "Bam!" while tossing spice powder in your face.
Cilantro	Smoke	The horrifying, crushing noise of Rick Bayless endlessly stepping on tortilla chips.
Curry powder	Freebase	Bollywood dance scenes with Padma Lakshmi; swimming in chicken tikka masala.
Dill	Mix with vinegar and inject intra-venously.	Enormous dancing pickles.
Ginger	Snort	Having a three-way with Ming Tsai and Martin Yan.
Mustard	Smoke	Attacked by giant hot dogs.
Paprika	Smoke	Running with chef José Andrés naked through the streets of Barcelona; Wolfgang Puck in a hot tub full of goulash.
Poppy seeds	Toast	Floating down the Hudson River on a giant poppy-seed bagel with Jackie Mason.
Rosemary	Smoke	Picking giant sunflowers with Jacques Pépin in Provence.
Tarragon	Smoke	Being chased by a fifty-foot-tall James Beard.

PASTA 2.0: NEW PASTA SHAPES

The Italians have a way with naming foods, and pastas are no exception. Many pasta shapes can refer to historical events, reflect cultural meanings, or slyly evoke everyday objects. One of the more famous might be *strozzapreti* ("priest-chokers"), not to mention *orecchiette*, the little bowl-shaped noodle that translates as "little ears," or *radiatori*, which are shaped like little radiators. Rising to the level of food poetry is the tortellini. The twisted, stuffed pasta supposedly evokes the bellybutton of Venus, the Roman goddess of love.

Unfortunately, there hasn't been much new in the arena of pasta design. In 1987, designer Philippe Starck came up with the *mandala* for French pasta maker Panzani. Referencing the Hindu and Buddhist art form, the *mandala* was designed with a unique shape engineered to compensate for overcooking. But it never took off.

So it's time that pasta got an update. Here are some concepts for entirely new pasta shapes that reflect the times we live in.

iPhonetti
Sleek, ultrathin, rectangular noodles that can communicate wirelessly with any sauce.

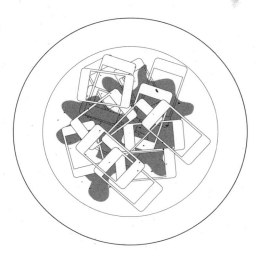

Recessionini

Evoking the tenuous state of the global economy, this spaghetti-like pasta is stretched by hand until thin, almost to the breaking point. Boil and serve dry without sauce.

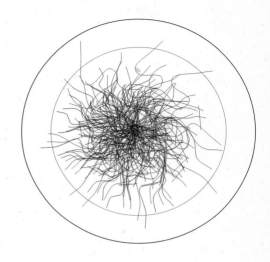

Cloonetti

Handsome ovals of pasta typically served with a dusting of salt and pepper.

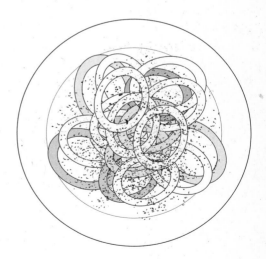

Wieneroni

A sheet of pasta formed into a beggar's purse bulging with a sausage filling. Although wieneroni was once served in the halls of Congress, it has since fallen out of favor.

Palini

A pasta that appears to be ravioli, but instead holds the empty promise of any actual filling. Pair with freshly killed moose Bolognese sauce.

Lohani
A modern take on
the tortellini, these
bellybutton-shaped
noodles are typically
dusted with cocaine
and fermented in wine
or other spirits. Eating
Lohani and driving is
not recommended
(appoint a designated
driver).

Bobbyflayette
Similar to penne, but
with faux grill marks
colored with squid ink.
Serve with *pico de gallo* and
a drizzle of Mexican *crema*.

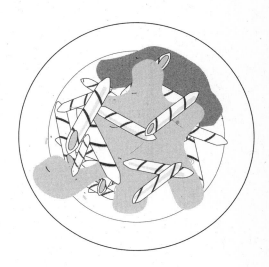

Batalini
Tiny orange clog-shaped
noodles. A favorite of
Gwyneth Paltrow.

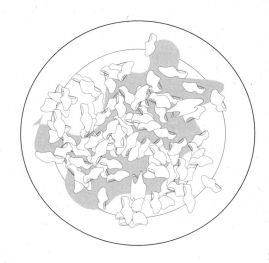

SUVette
Enormous, oversized
gnocchi that require
more than double the
amount of olive oil as
traditional recipes.

Twitteroni

This tiny bird-shaped pasta is typically made in 140-noodle servings. Leftover pasta can be refrigerated and retweeted.

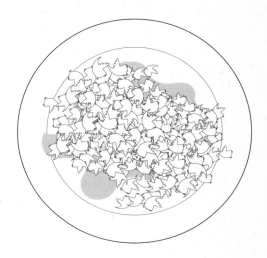

Kardashioni

While delicious, these pillowy, bottom-heavy noodles are known for being devoid of any nutritional value. Pair with dark meat.

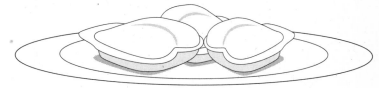

Hipsteroni

A local specialty of Williamsburg, Brooklyn, these beard-shaped noodles pair nicely with an ice-cold can of Pabst Blue Ribbon beer. If you can't make them yourself, they are available for mail order at etsy.com.

Kanyettini

Yo, spaghetti, I'm really happy for you and I'mma let you finish, but *kanyettini* is one of the best pastas of all time.

Twilightenne

The eternal struggle
between werewolves and
vampires is played out
in this pasta. *Twilightenne*
feature deep indentations
made by fork tines,
echoing Jacob the werewolf's
washboard abs. Pair with
a white-to-gray béchamel
sauce that evokes Edward
the vampire's ashen pallor.

Dharmette

Despite the disappointing
finale of the television
series *Lost,* this octagonal-
shaped pasta evoking
the Dharma Initiative
logo remains popular
with many nerds.

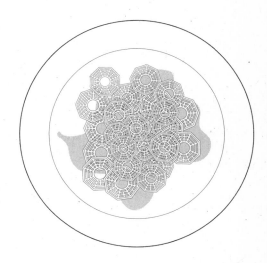

SO YOU WANT TO BE A . . . **Hipster Butcher**

Do you have the cojones to be a hipster butcher? Literally, do you have a good supplier of bull testicles? Because you're going to need them.

If you ever wanted to be a rock star but didn't have the musical "chops," now is your chance to court your own devoted fan base through the art of butchering and your skill at dividing animals into, well, chops.

		YES	NO
1	Do you know the difference between a hanger steak and a flat iron steak?		
2	Do you have a beard and/or handlebar mustache?		
3	Have you ever given a Brazilian bikini wax to a dead pig?		
4	Do hot chicks hang around outside your refrigerator?		
5	Do you live in Brooklyn or Portland?		
6	Is your LDL cholesterol level above 300?		
7	Do you have a tattoo of legendary Tuscan butcher Dario Cecchini on your lower back?		
8	In sixth grade, when your schoolmates dissected frogs, did you butcher them, instead?		
9	Do you prefer to listen to Johnny Cash when butchering a pig?		
10	Is it true you haven't eaten a boneless, skinless chicken breast in ten years?		

● **If you answered "yes" three times or fewer:**
You are not hipster butcher material. Have you considered becoming a vegan?

● **If you answered "yes" four to seven times:**
With the right amount of training, you might be able to remove the bone from a chicken thigh.

● **If you answered "yes" to eight or more questions:**
Congratulations! You have exactly what it takes to be a hipster butcher. Get ready for legions of fans, a devoted following, and countless women hungering for your prized tube steak.

FOOD-SAFETY CHECKLIST

With the startling increase in the number of meat and produce recalls in recent years and the looming risk of food-borne illnesses and bacterial contamination, there are a number of basic steps that you can take to ensure food safety in your own home.

☐ Leftovers kept in the refrigerator may be safely eaten for up to four days as a general rule. However, after forty-five days, you can make a delicious cocktail with all of the fermented juices.

☐ Always wash your hands with soap and warm water before handling ingredients. Then, wash all of your ingredients in pure bleach (always wear white).

☐ "Prewashed" lettuces typically contain the same amount of bacteria as a "prewashed" homeless person whose last shower was twelve months ago.

☐ Always turn a frying pan's handle away from the front of the stove, except when Guy Fieri is over.

☐ Canned goods with a bulging lid may indicate two things: (1) the possibility of spoilage, or (2) a very sexually aroused food product.

☐ In the event of a power outage, keep your foods safe by keeping the refrigerator and freezer doors closed at all times. Only open them in a bacon emergency.

HOLIDAY COOKING TIPS: BE A MASTER BASTER

There is a terror that strikes Americans every year. It's a level of anxiety greater than filing income taxes, making an appointment for a colonoscopy, or even meeting Thomas Keller for the first time. I'm referring, of course, to Thanksgiving.

Fear of a dry turkey seems to strike right at the heart of American patriotism. Did an epidemic of dry turkey cause the recent recession? We'll never know. But the odds are that it probably did.

But listen. Take a deep breath and realize there's absolutely nothing to worry about. Even if it's your first time boning a turkey, you need to relax. Turn down the lights, mix yourself (and the turkey) a cocktail, put on some soft jazz music, and let the boning take its natural course.

Before long, Thanksgiving cooking will become a no-brainer. Once you get the hang of it, you may even earn the much-heralded title of Master Baster:

Here are some simple tips to ensure a successful Thanksgiving feast.

» **Overcooking:** One of the big problems in roasting a turkey is that the white meat tends to cook much faster than the dark meat. As a result, in order to thoroughly cook the dark meat, you risk overcooking and drying out the white meat. One solution is to slow down the speed at which the white meat cooks. You can achieve this by icing down the breasts so they don't finish cooking before the thighs. But please be careful around the nipples. They are very sensitive.

» **Time-savers:** Did you sleep too late and forget to put the turkey in the oven? For a great Thanksgiving time-saver, try turkey sashimi. Or even worse, did you leave a frozen turkey in the freezer and forget to thaw it out? Hone a sharp knife and scrape the flesh to make Thanksgiving snow cones. Kids love them!

» **Self-basting:** Self-basting turkeys are no fun. Thanksgiving is a communal affair. Be a mutual master baster.

» **Moistness:** Rub a generous amount of butter on the breasts (you can also put some on the turkey, too, while you are at it). Also, don't overdo it trying to cook a moist bird. If the turkey is too moist, you may want to consult a gynecologist.

» **Turducken:** Try making a turducken as an alternative to the traditional turkey. After all, is there anything more erotic than boning a chicken, duck, and a turkey at one time? If turducken doesn't sound exciting enough, add a layer of foie gras to make a turfucken.

» **Giblets:** Don't forget, always fondle the giblets before you dress the turkey.

» **Boning:** When it comes to boning the bird, a nice drizzle of cream on the breasts to finish off is traditional.

» **Vegetarians:** If you're stuck with vegetarians as guests, you can serve them white meat, which is considered the "vegetables" of the turkey.

» **Brining:** Brining has become very popular for Thanksgiving. Get started by at least noon on the day of the feast so that you are completely brined by the time dinner starts.

ORGASMIC CHOCOLATE: FROM FOREPLAY TO CLIMAX

Surely you've tasted a chocolate Kiss, and perhaps you've heard people talk about chocolate that's "orgasmic." But sadly, you may have never witnessed, much less experienced, the extraordinarily sensual experience that is a chocolate orgasm. Chocolate "virgins" will find this handy guide essential to getting past first base with cacao.

» **Source**
Steer away from chocolates from Northern European countries. There's a reason that chocolates made in Scandinavia, for example, have a reputation for being "frigid." Avoid them.

» **Undressing**
Don't just tear off the wrapper like some kind of animal. Pour a glass of wine. Talk to the chocolate. Listen to what it has to say. Woo it. When the time is right, carefully fold back the paper without ripping. Feel free to get into bed with the chocolate, but keep in mind that the sheets can get awfully messy.

» **Foreplay**
A little foreplay doesn't hurt to move things along. When your chocolate contains cacao nibs, try gently tickling the nibs before moving on to the main act.

» **The Crying Game**
A word of advice to heterosexual men and to people with allergies: some chocolates may contain nuts. Proceed carefully.

» **Multiple Orgasms**
Yes, multiple orgasms are possible. For example, a twenty-four-piece box of chocolates can potentially result in twenty-four orgasms. I'm getting tired just thinking about it.

» **Race and Chocolate**
Not to unfairly discriminate against white chocolate, but, as the saying goes, once you go black, you never go back.

YOU ARE WHAT YOU EAT

The great gastronomic thinker Jean Anthelme Brillat-Savarin famously wrote, "Tell me what you eat, and I will tell you what you are." So, what exactly are you, anyway?

If you eat or drink . . .	You are probably . . .
Instant ramen	In college
Alizé	Slutty
Kale chips	Vegan
Prime rib	Old
Marrow bones	Intelligent
Cupcakes	Immature
Macaroni and cheese	In kindergarten
Moonshine	Drunk
Mice	A cat
Boneless, skinless chicken breasts	Depressed
Brains	A zombie
Beef consommé	Very old
Applesauce	Toothless
Awesome Blossoms	Suburban
French fries	Liberal
Freedom fries	Conservative

Nose to Tail or Tail to Nose? A Guide to Whole Beast Eating

Once you have embraced the whole-animal approach to eating, you
may never go back to eating chicken breasts again. But as simple as the
nose-to-tail eating mantra may sound, it's not always so easy in practice.
So before you get yourself accidentally tied up in a goat's small intestines,
please consult this handy guide:

1. **Pig**
   Nose to tail
   This one's a no-brainer. The über—"whole beast," pigs evolved over
   hundreds of thousands of years specifically so that humans could eat
   them from their snouts to their hairy little tails.

2. **Proboscis Monkey**
   Tail to nose
   Unlike the pig, the proboscis monkey's unusually large nose would
   be far too filling to start with. Instead, begin at the rear of the monkey
   and work your way toward the nose. *See also*: platypus.

3. **Eel**
   Anything goes
   The eel has long been a serious challenge for the whole-animal eater,
   particularly if you're drunk. "Which end is which?" is the common
   refrain of many intoxicated whole-eel eaters. *See also*: stingray,
   snake, starfish.

4. **Camel**

Nose to tail to hump

Start with the nose and then switch to the tail, saving the hump as the main course.

5. **Elephant**

Trunk to tail to ears

Nibble on the trunk as an appetizer, followed by the remainder of the body, saving the elephant ears for dessert, which are simply fantastic dusted with cinnamon and sugar.

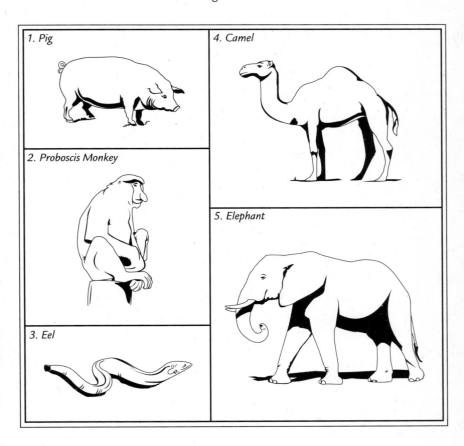

1. Pig

2. Proboscis Monkey

3. Eel

4. Camel

5. Elephant

6. Giraffe

Legs to neck to tail to head

In order not to fill up on the neck, it's recommended you start at the legs and work your way up, doubling back for the tail and finally on to the neck and head.

7. Kangaroo

Torso to nose to tail to pouch

This is fun at parties. Have someone blindfold you and put you inside the pouch. Your challenge is to eat your way out. Start with the torso, then consume the nose and tail, saving the actual pouch for last.

8. Turtle

Flip 'n' eat

God love 'em, turtles are the only animals that come with their own bowl. Simply turn the turtle over so that it's shell-side down and then eat with one of those serrated grapefruit spoons. Great for picnics.

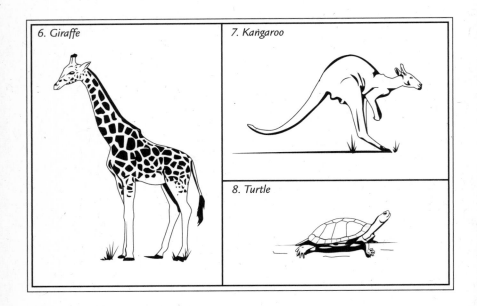

6. Giraffe

7. Kangaroo

8. Turtle

SHOULD YOU EAT THAT CHICKEN? A DECISION-MAKING FLOWCHART

There's a lot of confusion out there about food choices in the modern world. Is the food you choose to buy and cook for yourself and your loved ones safe to eat? Is it sustainable? Will it taste good?

Nothing can be more confounding to the modern eater than choosing the correct chicken to eat. A USDA ORGANIC label gives the consumer a degree of confidence, but ultimately you must personally weigh a number of variables—from the chicken's access to the outdoors to whether it was given any drugs or antibiotics, and if it ate a healthy diet—before making a safe, healthy, and tasty choice for your family. (See the Decision-Making Flowchart on page 160.)

This handy flowchart will give you the confidence to make the best choices with the right information.

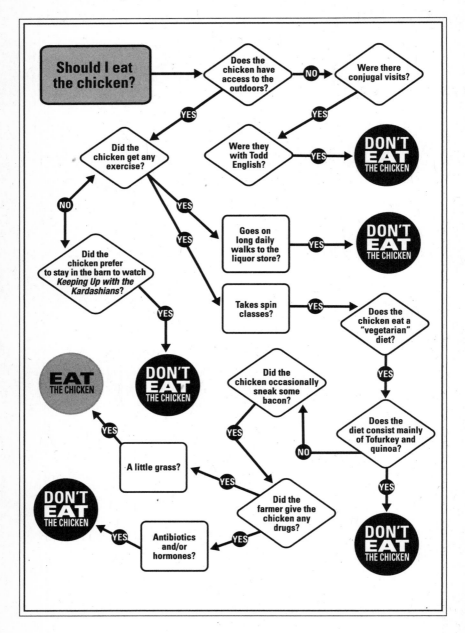

CHAPTER 6

The World of Wine and Spirits

The essentials of tasting wine and spirits,
understanding the language
of wine-speak, and pairing wine with food

"How I Learned to Stop Worrying and Love Hedonistic Fruit Bombs"

June 1982
SONOMA, California

"Would you like to see my fruit bomb?" he asked, which was weird since we'd only just met.

"Um, I guess so," I responded, suddenly noticing the tremendous bulge in his tight jeans.

And then, right in the middle of the vineyard—I couldn't believe what was happening—he unbuckled his belt, unzipped his pants, reached down, and pulled it out. Yikes! It was big, dark, and shiny, and it glistened in the sun. I don't think I'd ever seen one that big before.

"So, what do you think?" he said, pointing proudly at his prized possession. "A hundred points, I'd say!"

"Frankly, I have to tell you that I'm a little freaked out by the size of that thing," I confessed. "In all my years, I've just never seen one that massive."

"It's a bottle of wine called a jeroboam," he boasted. "Four and a half fucking liters, baby!"

"That's a lot of alcohol," I said.

"Fuck yeah! Total hedonism!" he boomed. "In fact, this thing is fifteen percent alcohol! That's how I roll!"

I went back to my car to grab a couple of wineglasses, but when I got back he yanked them out of my hands and tossed them into the vineyard.

"We don't need no stinking glasses!" he bellowed as they smashed against the ground.

The next thing I knew, he took me in his arms, laid me down in the narrow space between two rows of vines, caressed my chin, and tipped the massive bottle of wine into my mouth. And that was my last memory of the night I spent with the famous wine critic Robert Parker.

HOW TO TASTE A GLASS OF WINE

Tasting a glass of wine can be daunting to the uninitiated. If you've only used a sippy cup, brace yourself for a complex, challenging, but ultimately intoxicating (literally!) ride. Once you get the hang of tasting wine you will soon become a pro. Just follow this three-step process and, before you know it, you can call yourself a real connoisseur (though you might find it hard to say "connoisseur" without slurring).

» **LOOK:** Pour a glass of wine into the appropriate wineglass. Depending on the wine and your mood, you may want to choose a smaller glass suitable for white wines, a larger glass for rosés, or a leftover Big Gulp container for heavy-bodied red wines.

» **OVERALL IMPRESSION:** Without leering, check it out. Don't gawk, but don't be too shy, either. Is it cute, hot, sexy, demure? Is it nasty, skeezy, boring? Would you take it on a date? Would you introduce it to your mom? Is this a "relationship wine" or more of a "one-night-stand wine"? Maybe you could just be friends. Or maybe there's the possibility of "friends with benefits."

» **COLOR:** What color is it? If it's a red wine, would you say it's the color of a just-bludgeoned mafia don? Or perhaps it has the brownish hues of a soiled diaper. If it's a white wine, would you say it is a pale yellow, like pee after drinking two six-packs of lager, or more of a light-green asparagus pee?

» **LEGS:** Swirling the wine leaves behind streaks on the inside of the glass known as the wine's "legs," which some feel is an indicator of wine quality. After swirling, it's typical to comment on how the legs look. Here are some examples from some of the world's most highly regarded wine critics:

> "Great gams!"
> "Haven't seen legs this great since Beyonce's 'Single Ladies' video."
> "This cabernet is amazing: She's got legs, and she knows how to use them."

» **SMELL**: This is one of the most important stages of tasting wine. Carefully follow these four steps:

1. **Nads**: Not to be confused with "legs" (see page 163), the nads are typically only fondled during tasting very heavy-bodied, high-testosterone red wines. Rub the glass at the spot where the base of the "bowl" meets the stem of the glass. Do this rhythmically and rapidly for a few minutes while coaxing the wine along with supportive phrases like, "this feels so good" or "you're almost there." This will gradually raise the temperature of the wine until reaching an aromatic explosion. After the wine reaches climax, smoke a cigarette.

2. **Snorting**: Resting your nose directly on the rim, snort deeply and loudly. Be careful to avoid getting any wine in your brain, however. What do you smell? Do you smell oak, fruit, a homeless man's socks? How about vanilla, citrus, or car exhaust? Are there notes of leather or do you smell vinyl? Do you smell coffee tones? Be specific: Decaf half-cap or hazelnut Frappuccino?

3. **Total Immersion**: Now pour more wine into the glass until it reaches the rim. Carefully immerse your nose completely in the wine. How does it feel? Can your nose do the backstroke? Can it float unassisted? Now exhale through your nose. Does it make bubbles? Isn't that cool? Show your mom how cool it is.

4. **Nasal Irrigation**: also known as wine douching. Pour the wine into a neti pot and insert the spout into one nostril at a time, flushing the wine through your nasal passages and letting it drain out of the other nostril. Save the spent wine for the sommelier. Did it clear up your congestion? Wine douching is highly recommended during the spring allergy season.

TASTE: Congratulations! You got through the smell test with flying colors! You've arrived at my favorite portion of the tasting: the drinking phase. Follow these three crucial steps and bottoms up!

1. **The Attack Phase:** Get in a "wine stance" with both feet planted on the ground, chest forward, knees slightly bent, and arms astride. Without warning, lunge at the wineglass, grabbing it by the stem firmly with your right hand and covering the top with your left palm so no wine escapes and then pin the glass to the floor. The attack is composed of four variables: tannin levels, acidity, residual sugar, and will-it-fuck-you-up-edness. This can be a very physical struggle to ascertain these characteristics, so be prepared to do whatever it takes: roundhouse kicks, sucker punches, lying, crying, scratching, and clawing. Waterboarding may be necessary for the boldest varietals.

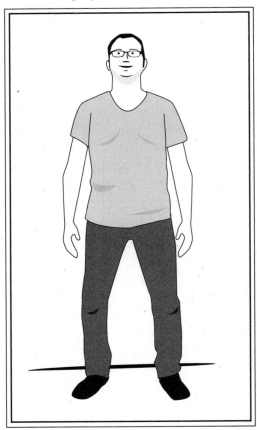

2. **The Evolution Phase:** Following the attack phase, the wine should completely submit to your authority. The good news is after all the other nonsense that came before, you are finally going to actually drink the wine. Also known as the mid palate or middle range of a wine tasting, this phase helps you assess the wine's taste. If it's a red wine you may start noting fruit: berry, plum, prune, or Jujubes. Maybe you taste spice: pepper, clove, cinnamon, or tomatillo salsa. Is there a woody flavor like oak, cedar, or back porch? If you're tasting a white wine, you might taste apple, honey, citrus, or urinal. There might be a hint of earthiness, or maybe you taste Uranus. If so, spit it out in the sommelier's hand.

3. **The Finish:** not to be confused with the "money shot," which is professional lingo specific to champagne tastings when the sommelier sprays bubbly on the taster's chest. Rather, the finish is the final phase of tasting a glass of wine. How long does the flavor impression last after it's swallowed? Do you regret not putting a condom on the wineglass? Did you achieve winegasm? Were there multiple winegasms? Was it light bodied (like the consistency of water), medium bodied (think milk), or full bodied (the consistency of Oprah)? Is there an aftertaste? Do you want another sip? Would you stay the night, or do you feel like you should get dressed and go home? On the other hand, if you really liked the wine but the wine didn't call you the next day, would you stay in bed and cry?

RUTH'S RULES

It is perfectly fine to drink wine with cork taint
so long as it smells better than your own taint.

AN INTRODUCTION TO WINE-SPEAK

When traveling to a foreign country, you always prepare for encountering people who speak another language. Whether that means taking a language class or picking up a phrasebook, you need to be ready to speak a language that is not your own. The same goes for the world of wine. Oenophiles speak a highly obscure language called *wine-speak*, which includes its own unique grammar, syntax, and vocabulary.

The Tasting Note: A Dissection

Here's a typical tasting note, an example of wine-speak as used by wine critic James Molesworth to describe Laurent Fayolle Hermitage White Les Dionnières 2009 for *Wine Spectator*. Notice the overuse of adjectives, wordy phrasing, racial fantasies, and hints of the critic's morbid curiosities:

The wine evokes the flavor of Paris Hilton.

Code word for a wine that's a little bit gay, not that there's anything wrong with that

"Rich yet racy, with distinctive Asian pear, white peach and chamomile notes backed by a long finish of salted butter. Shows nice buried minerality."

Subtle racial coding to indicate this wine will be favored by white guys with an Asian fetish

Giveaway that the critic wrote these tasting notes while eating breakfast toast (see also: "evocative of Cheerios"). Ignore this.

Classic example of necrophilia. A lot of wine critics are into that.

WINE WORDS: A CHEAT SHEET

In order to read tasting notes and even create your own, you need to learn wine vocabulary. Unfortunately, the words typically used in wine-speak have become trite, clichéd, and largely ineffective at accurately describing the complex characteristics of wine. Try replacing these stodgy wine terms with more up-to-date and accurate descriptions:

Wine characteristic	Typical wine-speak	Alternative wine-speak
A wine that will benefit from further maturation	Ageworthy	Bieberesque
A wine that feels full and generous	Ample	Kardashian
Wines perfumed with strong scents	Aromatic	Snortable
A wine that makes a major impression, usually full bodied, or a wine with intense aroma or plenty of flavor	Big	Long Dong Silvery
A heavy, intense, and complex red wine	Brooding	Harrison Fordish
A wild yeast that occasionally afflicts wines, sometimes giving off a fecal odor	Brett	Pinched a loaf
The smell and taste of wines matured in oak barrels	Buttery	Got wood?
Flavors that remind one of the smell of cedar wood	Cedary	Grandma's closety
A scent of tobacco, typical of some Bordeaux	Cigar box	Castro-like
Hidden	Cloaked	Jedi
Spoiled wine	Corked	Sale binnish
After some time, an ageworthy wine (see above) that shows little complexity from aging	Dumb	Jessica Simpsonian

Wine characteristic	Typical wine-speak	Alternative wine-speak
Some red wines have an earthy, musky taste.	Earthy	New York City cab driver
A simple wine that can be enjoyed as it is, without much consideration as to its attributes	Easy-Drinking	Slutty
Firm, balanced, and well defined (the opposite of flabby)	Finesse	Michelle Obama's arms
Aromas suggestive of herbs	Herbal	Bongworthy
Another take on "earthy," often found in older red wines	Leather	Whip it good!
The winemaking process by which the phenolic materials of the grape (tannins, coloring agents, and flavor compounds) are leached from the grape skins, seeds, and stems	Maceration	Stroking the vine
Lively, spirited, crisp, stimulating	Racy	Good in bed
The flavor and aroma of sulphur, an antioxidant introduced in some wines	Sulphurized	Farty
Smoothness, often used to describe red Burgundy and other pinot noir	Velvety	Barry Whiteish

THE ART OF WINE PAIRING

Pairing wine with foods is one of the most complicated and challenging aspects of gastronomy. In the Middle Ages, wine pairing was actually considered to be a "dark art" and was only practiced by wizards. Over time, wine pairing has entered the mainstream. But even today, there are vestiges of its cultlike origins. Read any wine magazine or check out the wine section of a bookstore and you will still find shamanlike "wine critics" professing almost divine knowledge of how to match wines with foods. Don't bother with these megalomaniacs. Here's all you need to know when it comes to wine pairings:

» **Color:** There's no need to stick to rigid rules when pairing wines with meats, but red wines tend to pair well with red meats and white wines are typically best matched with fish. Try rosé wines with undercooked chicken.

» **Synergy:** Look for symmetry between wines and foods. A big, round, juicy burger always pairs well with *Kardashian* reds. Similarly, lean meats pair nicely with wines that exhibit the character of *Michelle Obama's arms*.

» **Opposites:** On the other hand, go for contrast. Pair sophisticated cheeses with *Jessica Simpsonian* wines or a dry-aged ribeye with something *Bieberesque*. Be inventive!

» **Mood:** Don't ruin the aphrodisiac powers of oysters with a wine that smells like a *New York City cab driver*. Go for something *slutty* to keep the sexual energy alive.

» **Weight:** Match the weight of food with wine. Pour a glass of wine and then dunk some of your food in the wine. If it sinks, it's a match. But if it floats, choose an alternative. This is why it's so challenging to find wines that pair well with popcorn.

SO YOU WANT TO BE A . . . **Wine Critic**

Becoming a wine critic requires a rigorous commitment to understanding the winemaking process, differentiating between myriad wine varietals, having strict dental hygiene, and refining the art of spitting. Do you have what it takes to become a wine ~~snob~~ expert?

		YES	NO
1	Do you get angry about merlot?		
2	Would you describe the color of your teeth as "rosé"?		
3	When you hear someone talking about a "full-bodied red," do you always get thirsty and never aroused?		
4	Have you ever woken up with a cork in your underpants?		
5	Is it true you've never giggled when hearing or saying the word "pinot"?		
6	As a six-year-old child, did you once describe apple juice as having "notes of honeyed peach, pineapple, and candied tangerine, balanced by a tangy acidity and a floral, slightly almondy finish"?		
7	Is it true you no longer own white shirts?		
8	Do you pair Cheerios with white wines, but Cocoa Puffs with red wines?		
9	Do you find beer connoisseurs insufferable?		
10	Do you think corkage fees are totally acceptable?		

● **If you answered "yes" three times or fewer:**
You don't have the makings for a career as a wine critic. You may still get drunk on wine, however.

● **If you answered "yes" four to seven times:**
You are not wine critic material, but you have the skills needed to make a great sommelier.

● **If you answered "yes" to eight or more questions:**
Congratulations! You have what it takes to be ~~the most annoying person in the restaurant industry~~ a wine critic. Cheers!

THAT'S THE SPIRIT: A GUIDE TO THE HARD STUFF

Setting up your home bar needn't be a huge investment. You can easily get started with a gallon of vodka and a straw. (You may need to expand your arsenal to include a spoon—straw if you're making frozen cocktails.) But for more advanced mixology, you will need to gain a basic understanding of cocktail-mixing principles and acquire some essential tools to equip your bar.

» **Storing Your Liquor**: Liquor should keep for plenty of time, provided it is kept in a cool, dark place away from direct sunlight. One of the pluses of living in a cave is that you can keep your liquor right out in the open. That's why bears have it so good (and why they are able to sleep so long during hibernation).

» **Barware Basics**: You don't need a lot of fancy equipment to equip your bar, but there are some tools that make mixology easier. (Ever try muddling with a toothpick? Don't.) Here's a list of must-haves:

> Ice bag
> Muddler
> Jigger
> Cocktail shaker
> Strainer
> Ice cube trays
> Hypodermic needles
> Brass knuckles
> Razor blades
> Finger puppets

» **Glassware:** You should have four to eight of each of the following types of glassware: a short "rocks" glass, a tall "highball" glass, and a stem "martini" glass. I also like to have a few buckets on hand and a package of disposable barf bags.

» **Liquors:** Don't bother stocking your bar with dozens of bottles you'll never touch (unless you have just been diagnosed with clinical depression, in which case you'll need everything you can get your hands on). But there are some essentials:

> *Absinthe:* For drinking according to the traditional method using sugar and iced water, making smoothies (see recipe on page 176), and for hallucinating.
> *White Rum:* For mojitos, daiquiris, and pretending you are Ernest Hemingway.
> *Gin:* For martinis, gin and tonics, Tom Collinses, and variations on the Collins theme (see "The Collins Family of Cocktails" on page 177).
> *Bourbon:* For drinking straight, Old-Fashioneds, and reenacting scenes from *Mad Men* in your living room.
> *Vodka:* For screwdrivers, vodka tonics, and general inebriation.

RUTH'S RULES

When it comes to pairings, wine and cheese make for a lousy match. Introduce crackers for a crunchy and sensual three-way.

Recipe: How to Make an Absinthe Smoothie

Where as the typical smoothie, bursting with fresh fruit, can be a great pick-me-up, the Absinthe Smoothie is more of a pick-me-down. It's still a great way to start your day, provided your day involves lots of lying down and hallucinating.

Ingredients
4 ounces absinthe
1 scoop vanilla ice cream
2 cups ice
2 tablespoons sugar
1 tablespoon protein powder or cocaine, depending upon mood
Pinch of saffron

Preparation
Place all the ingredients in a blender at high speed for 1 minute. Add additional absinthe if the smoothie is too thick. If the mixture is too thin, add more ice cream. Pour into chilled glasses and garnish with psilocybin mushrooms and a slice of foie gras.

BASIC COCKTAIL TECHNIQUES

Rimming a Glass: One of the most erotic techniques in the bartender's arsenal. Sweet-talk the bartender into lying down behind the bar, invert the glass, and hold it in front of his or her mouth while he or she sensually licks the glass. Turn the glass right side up and proceed with mixing the cocktail.

Making a Twist: This is where two or more bartenders play a game of Twister while balancing a jigger of vodka on each of their heads. The first one to spill loses.

Flaming a Twist: The same as Making a Twist, only with two gay bartenders.

Smacking Herbs: Bartenders will "smack" herbs—smashing them between their hands over a drink—to release their essential oils. This is not to be confused with "smoking herb" (smoking marijuana) or "slapping the mint" (masturbation).

The Collins Family of Cocktails

The recipe for the original Tom Collins first appeared in the 1876 edition of *The Bartender's Guide*. It's a classic cocktail that combines gin, lemon juice, sugar, and club soda stirred together in a tall "Collins" glass. However, there are some lesser-known Collins variations that also deserve your attention:

» **Judy Collins**

This folksy variation, named for 1960s singer and social activist Judy Collins, follows the original recipe along with a dash of patchouli oil and a pinch of hashish.

» **Joan Collins**

Considered to be one of the bitchiest cocktails ever made, this version, named for the actress who starred as Alexis Carrington in the 1980s serial *Dynasty*, includes wasabi, bitters, Tabasco sauce, and a spritz of hair spray.

» **Phil Collins**

The singer Phil Collins is a lightning rod in music circles, and so is this cocktail, which is hated by many but also admired by some for its virtuosity. Whatever the case may be, it contains four times the amount of gin as the original Tom Collins, so after drinking one you'll be slurring so much that everything that comes out of your mouth will sound like "Sussudio."

» **Bootsy Collins**

Named for bassist, singer, and songwriter Bootsy Collins, this is one of the funkiest cocktails ever crafted. It includes all of the traditional ingredients for a Tom Collins along with an ounce of funk *and* an ounce of mojo. Always wear crazy sunglasses while mixing a Bootsy Collins and, instead of using a Collins glass, serve in an inverted sequined top hat.

SOME SEX ON THE BEACH VARIATIONS

You may be familiar with Sex on the Beach, the hugely popular yet disgusting spring-break libation believed to have originated in 1987, in Ft. Lauderdale, Florida. It is typically made with vodka, peach schnapps, orange juice, and cranberry juice. Over the past twenty-five years, a number of regional variations have emerged:

Classic Sex on the Beach

1½ oz vodka
½ oz peach schnapps

2 oz cranberry juice
2 oz orange juice

Add vodka and peach schnapps to a highball glass over ice. Fill with equal measures of cranberry and orange juice and stir.

Sex on the East River

1½ oz vodka
½ oz peach schnapps
2 oz cranberry juice

2 oz orange juice
1 dead body part
2 oz human feces

Add vodka and peach schnapps to a highball glass over feces. Fill with equal measures of cranberry juice and orange juice, and stir with the dead body part.

Sex on the Beach of Guantánamo Bay

1½ oz vodka
½ oz peach schnapps
2 oz cranberry juice

2 oz orange juice
1 rag

Add all the liquid ingredients to a cocktail mixer and shake. Saturate the rag with the cocktail mixture and serve the rag stuffed directly into the mouth. Pour additional cocktail mix over the rag as needed.

Sex on Chernobyl

1½ oz vodka
½ oz peach schnapps
2 oz cranberry juice

2 oz orange juice
2 oz enriched uranium

Add vodka and peach schnapps to a cocktail glass over uranium. Fill with equal measures of cranberry and orange juice and shake until glowing.

COCKTAIL LINGO: A CHEAT SHEET

Like wine connoisseurs, bartenders have their own peculiar language and code words for talking about cocktails and the techniques for making and serving them. Use this guide as a cheat sheet for all of your mixological needs:

Neat: a drink served without ice, not mixed or chilled.

Felix Unger: a customer who only orders "neat" drinks.

Muddle: mashing ingredients, such as citrus, to release their juices and essential oils.

Meddle: muddling in inappropriate places.

Mittell: muddling in Germany.

Soldier: a full beer bottle.

Drone: an empty beer bottle thrown at the bartender.

Shot: typically, a one- to two-ounce serving of a single type of spirit.

Vaccine: typically, a one- to two-ounce serving of a single type of spirit taken intravenously.

Splash: approximately ½ teaspoon.

Belly Flop: approximately four ounces.

On the Rocks: a drink poured over one's testicles.

Rocks Off: a cocktail with a squirt of Bailey's Irish Cream.

Hair of the Dog: a drink that is supposed to be a cure for hangovers.

Hair of the Cat: a drink that may cause hairballs.

Hair of the Coke Can: a peculiar favorite of Supreme Court Justice Clarence Thomas.

Barfly: one who frequents a bar.

Barfry: a barfly who always orders french fries.

Chimneyfish: a barfly who "drinks like a fish" and "smokes like a chimney."

Jiminy Cricket: a barfly who eats too many *chapulines* (toasted grasshoppers) at a Mexican bar.

Brezhnester: a Russian barfly who stays all night and drinks only vodka.

Appendix

What's your GQ?

Are you a foodie? Take this simple questionnaire to find your gastronomical quotient (GQ), which measures your culinary knowledge, gastronomical prowess, and gustatory morality.

Choose one answer for each question and tabulate your final score according to the answer key on page 189. With any luck, you'll discover your GQ is downright "Kellerian." My condolences if you discover you are "Velveetan."

Multiple Choice

1) You are home alone on a Saturday night and hungry. You whip up:
   a. Box of macaroni and cheese
   b. Heat-and-serve chicken nuggets
   c. Pan-roasted duck breasts, fingerling potatoes, and baby root vegetables
   d. Instant ramen
   e. Bowl of cereal

2) You are on a desert island with a subscription to one major food magazine. Which is it?
   a. *Saveur*
   b. *Food Network Magazine*
   c. *Vegetarian Times*
   d. *Every Day with Rachael Ray*
   e. *Cooking Light*

3) Every Christmas, you cross your fingers and hope you'll receive:
   a. A *sous-vide* machine
   b. McDonald's gift certificates
   c. Omaha steaks
   d. A George Foreman Lean Mean Grilling Machine
   e. A nonstick skillet

4) Your preferred coffee drink is:
   a. Espresso
   b. Pumpkin spice–flavored coffee
   c. Frappuccino
   d. Sanka
   e. Decaf latte

5) You would most likely buy a cookbook from which of the following celebrity chefs?
   a. Thomas Keller
   b. Paula Deen
   c. Emeril Lagasse
   d. Tyler Florence
   e. Sandra Lee

6) You are traveling by interstate highway and must stop for a quick meal. Rank the following five chains in order of preference from best option to worst option: McDonald's, Chick-Fil-A, Roy Rogers, Chipotle, In-N-Out. Which of the following most closely matches your own rank order?

a. Roy Rogers, McDonald's, Chick-Fil-A, In-N-Out, Chipotle
b. In-N-Out, Chick-Fil-A, Chipotle, McDonald's, Roy Rogers
c. Chick-Fil-A, McDonald's, Roy Rogers, In-N-Out, Chipotle
d. Chipotle, McDonald's, Chick-Fil-A, Roy Rogers, In-N-Out
e. McDonald's, Chipotle, Roy Rogers, Chick-Fil-A, In-N-Out

7) You or your spouse has just given birth to your first child, a boy. You name him:
a. Ferran
b. Emeril
c. Rocco
d. Guy
e. Chef Boyardee

8) Your most trusted kitchen tool is a:
a. Garlic press
b. Food processor
c. Chef's knife
d. Slap Chop
e. Microwave oven

9) Your favorite TV chef is:
a. Rachael Ray
b. The Swedish Chef
c. Tom Colicchio
d. Paula Deen
e. Giada De Laurentiis

10) At a dinner party you are hosting, one of your guests tells you that your Italian cooking is almost as good as the Olive Garden. Which of the following would be an appropriate way of responding?
a. Cry and stab yourself with *perciatelli*.
b. Call her a douchebaguette.
c. Feign ignorance: "Is that a new restaurant? I haven't been."
d. Defriend her on Facebook.
e. All of the above.

11) Your favorite food shop is:
a. Safeway
b. Whole Foods
c. Eataly
d. Trader Joe's
e. Target "Greatland"

12) You tend to avoid restaurants that specialize in:
a. Seasonal menus
b. Wines served by the *quartino*
c. Deep-fried blooming onions
d. Yakitori
e. Heritage meats

13) Which of the following items are you unlikely to find in your refrigerator?
a. Sriracha
b. American cheese slices
c. Salt-packed anchovies
d. Fish sauce
e. Shallots

14) Your favorite "food movie" is:
   a. *Eat, Pray, Love*
   b. *Tampopo*
   c. *Mystic Pizza*
   d. *Chocolat*
   e. *American Pie*

15) Food you claim to enjoy but secretly despise:
   a. Bacon
   b. Steak
   c. Pork belly
   d. Okra
   e. Cheese

16) Food you claim to despise but secretly enjoy:
   a. Pop-Tarts
   b. Sweetbreads
   c. Venison
   d. Pasta
   e. Veggie burgers

17) You are committed to organic, local, seasonal, and sustainable cuisine, except when dining in _____ restaurants.
   a. Chinese
   b. Mexican
   c. Vietnamese
   d. Korean
   e. All of the above

18) When it comes to appliances, you prefer a(n) _____ range, and a(n) _____ oven.
   a. gas; gas
   b. gas; electric
   c. electric; gas
   d. electric; electric

19) What's the most important quality you look for when purchasing chicken?
   a. USDA ORGANIC LABEL
   b. Free range
   c. Vegetarian diet
   d. Inner beauty
   e. Big breasts

20) You are a member of:
   a. Costco
   b. Sam's Club
   c. Slow Food
   d. PETA
   e. TGI Friday's Frequent Diner Club

21) When shopping for steak, which cut are you most likely to choose?
   a. Skirt
   b. Hanger
   c. Rib Eye
   d. Strip
   e. Tenderloin

22) Celebrity chef Mario Batali has been a major influence on:
   a. The adoption of offal and other less popular meat cuts by Americans
   b. The spread of regional Italian cuisines
   c. The acceptance of Italian food in a fine-dining context
   d. The acceptability of wearing children's footwear by adult men
   e. All of the above

23) Chefs who work in the field of "molecular gastronomy" prefer to be called:
    a. Molecular gastronomists
    b. Food wizards
    c. Doctors of yum
    d. Modernists
    e. Tasteologists

24) You are against _____, but for _____.
    a. factory farming; foie gras
    b. mustard on hot dogs; ketchup
    c. young wines; Justin Bieber
    d. dark meat; white meat
    e. anchovies; red snapper

25) A knife with a "full tang" has
    a. Minimal taint
    b. Very large private parts
    c. Been endorsed by NASA
    d. A blade that extends the full length of the knife, including all the way through the handle
    e. All of the above

Analogies

26) Guy Fieri: Douchebaggery
    a. Thomas Keller: Finesse
    b. Paula Deen: Low-fat
    c. Rachael Ray: Skillful
    d. James Beard: Anorexia
    e. Burger King: Big Mac

27) Gordon Ramsay: Relaxed
    a. Bacon: Salty
    b. Cupcakes: Sweet
    c. Durian: Smelly
    d. Dogs: Feline
    e. Champagne: Bubbly

28) Celebrity chefs: Bald
    a. Liquids: Solid
    b. Birds: Feathered
    c. Einstein: Stupid
    d. Sarah Palin: Qualified
    e. Butter: Low-fat

29) Truffle oil: Truffles
    a. Cheese: Milk
    b. Steak: Cholesterol
    c. French fries: Potatoes
    d. Pamela Anderson: Real breasts
    e. Olive oil: Olives

30) White meat: Dark meat
    a. Stout: Light beer
    b. Prosciutto: SPAM
    c. Wine: Wine coolers
    d. Sea salt: Table salt
    e. Velveeta: Mozzarella

31) Chilean sea bass: Sustainable
    a. Rachael Ray: Annoying
    b. Food trucks: Trendy
    c. Per Se: Haute
    d. Bacon: Smoked
    e. Todd English: Pudgy

32) Extra-Virgin: Olive Oil
   a. Awesome: Blossom
   b. Prime: Steak
   c. Hangover: Absinthe
   d. Prudish: Safflower oil
   e. McDonald's: Burgers

33) Ferran Adrià: Molecular gastronomy
   a. Thomas Keller: Fast food
   b. Jacques Pépin: Mixology
   c. Jon Voight: Angelina Jolie
   d. Rick Bayless: California cuisine
   e. Sandra Lee: Farm to table

34) Mixology: Bartending
   a. Baking: Grilling
   b. Barbecuing: Steaming
   c. Salisbury steak: Hamburger
   d. Boiling: Simmering
   e. Eating: Drinking

35) Sandra Lee: Artisanal
   a. Rachael Ray: Quick
   b. Bobby Flay: Grilled
   c. Wolfgang Puck: Austrian
   d. Alice Waters: Processed
   e. Ina Garten: Barefoot

Reading Comprehension

36) In a review of the Mark Restaurant by Jean-Georges, former *New York Times* restaurant critic Sam Sifton offered the following description of Vongerichten's pea soup: "Also recycled, pleasantly, is the pea soup, a purée of sweet green peas that taste of springtime and have the smooth texture of high-thread-count sheets; a version of it exists on the tasting menu at Jean Georges, Mr. Vongerichten's four-star flagship near Columbus Circle. Blend in the accompanying cloud of Parmesan foam, and it's like a lover sliding into bed: nice." Which of the following conclusions can be made based upon reading this passage?

   a. Eating Vongerichten's pea soup is uncannily similar to having sex with Martha Stewart at her Skylands summer home in Maine.

   b. The pea soup is a very smooth blend of fresh sweet green peas topped with Parmesan.

   c. God, it's lonely being a restaurant critic. Mr. Sifton will gladly take companionship from cheese foam at this point in his career.

   d. Mr. Sifton really needs a new set of sheets.

   e. All of the above

37) In his 2011 book *The Table Comes First: Family, France, and the Meaning of Food*, *New Yorker* staff writer Adam Gopnik writes: "A kind of primal scene of eating hovers over every cookbook, just as a primal scene of sex lurks behind every love story. In cooking, the primal scene, or substance, is salt, sugar,

and fat held in maximum solution with starch; add protein as necessary and finish with caffeine (coffee or chocolate) as desired." Which of the following conclusions can be made based upon reading this statement?

a. Mr. Gopnik reads his cookbooks in the nude.
b. Mr. Gopnik once had a three-way with *Mastering the Art of French Cooking* and *The Joy of Cooking*.
c. Mr. Gopnik's orgasms contain high doses of caffeine.
d. All of the above

38) In the following passage from her book *A Homemade Life,* blogger and author Molly Wizenberg describes her preference for scones: "When something clicks with me, I want to keep it around. That goes not only for recipes but also for facial cleansers, chocolate, and men. But about the recipes. My sister Lisa's Scottish scones are another good example. I prefer scones over all other morning breads, and of the specimens I have sampled, hers are my very favorite." Based upon your reading of this passage, which of the following assumptions can be made about Wizenberg and her sister's scones?

a. The scones, like her facial cleansers, are suited for people with normal to dry skin.
b. Wizenberg likes her scones the same way she likes her men: rich, buttery, and Scottish.
c. The scones are made with chocolate. Hence, if life is like a box of chocolates, then you will never know what kind of scones you're going to get.
d. All of the above

39) In his review of the restaurant Marea, former *New York Times* restaurant critic Sam Sifton made the following observation about one of the appetizers: "The very first item on the menu at Marea is ricci, a piece of warm toast slathered with sea urchin roe, blanketed in a thin sheet of lardo, and dotted with sea salt. It offers exactly the sensation as kissing an extremely attractive person for the first time—a bolt of surprise and pleasure combined. The salt and fat give way to primal sweetness and combine in deeply agreeable ways. The feeling lingers on the tongue and vibrates through the body." Which of the following conclusions can be made based on this passage?

a. Mr. Sifton is into vibrators.
b. Sea urchin roe is not only delicious but looks really hot.
c. When kissing Mr. Sifton, always wear sea salt—flavored lip gloss.
d. Mr. Sifton sleeps on sheets made of *lardo*.
e. All of the above

40) In her recipe for saltimbocca, food writer Amanda Hesser provides the following instructions on pounding veal: "Between sheets of wax paper or parchment, pound the veal cutlets, one at a time, until very thin (⅛ inch). They should be the size of a woman's shoe. Cover each cutlet with a slice of prosciutto and then two sage leaves. Fold the veal in half and secure shut with a toothpick. Season each veal package with a tiny bit of salt and plenty of pepper." Which of the following conclusions can be drawn based on an interpretation of this passage?

    a. Always pound veal with a woman's shoe.
    b. In a pinch, a veal cutlet can be worn as a flip-flop.
    c. Single men who attempt this recipe for saltimbocca should own a meat pounder and at least one pair of women's shoes.
    d. Ms. Hesser's veal cutlets may have scuff marks.
    e. All of the above

True/False

41) Washed-rind cheeses are dishwasher safe.
    a. True
    b. False

42) Pimiento del Piquillo is a Dominican baseball player who plays shortstop for the New York Mets.
    a. True
    b. False

43) You have eaten at one of chef David Chang's Momofuku restaurants.
    a. True
    b. False

44) You have eaten at Applebee's.
    a. True
    b. False

45) You can describe a wine as being "flaccid" with a straight face.
    a. True
    b. False

46) The 2009 film *Julie & Julia* was a sequel to the 1982 film *Victor/Victoria*.
   a. True
   b. False

47) When talking about chocolate, you call the beans "cacao" as opposed to "cocoa."
   a. True
   b. False

48) You have tried your hand at making your own bacon.
   a. True
   b. False

49) Alice Waters once turned heads by saying that for her last meal, she'd like to eat a bowl of shark fin soup.
   a. True
   b. False

50) Wolfgang Puck has not been outside of a QVC studio since 1992.
   a. True
   b. False

Answer Key

To score your GQ, give yourself one point for each correct answer.

1) c	11) c	21) a	31) e	41) b
2) a	12) c	22) e	32) b	42) b
3) a	13) b	23) d	33) c	43) a
4) a	14) b	24) a	34) c	44) b
5) a	15) d	25) d	35) d	45) a
6) b	16) a	26) a	36) e	46) b
7) a	17) e	27) d	37) d	47) a
8) c	18) b	28) b	38) d	48) a
9) c	19) a	29) d	39) e	49) a
10) e	20) c	30) e	40) e	50) a

Assessing Your GQ: After tabulating your total score, you can determine your gastronomical quotient.

0–10 points: VELVEETAN
Limited knowledge of gastronomy. Seek meaning and connection in nacho-cheese sauce. Exhibit loyalty to chef Guy Fieri and skepticism about eating beef cheeks. Thorough, painstaking, and accurate when making instant ramen.

11–30 points: EMERILIAN
Some familiarity with gastronomy, but mostly derived from watching the Food Network. Quiet, friendly, and conscientious about cleaning their George Foreman Lean Mean Grilling Machines. Take pleasure in saying "Bam!" when cooking. Notice and remember specific catchphrases of Rachael Ray. Strive to cook frozen pizzas properly without burning them.

31–40 points: BATALIAN
Strong knowledge of gastronomy. Curious about cured meats and quick to see the culinary possibilities of *lardo*. Adaptable, flexible, and accepting, unless their truffles are threatened. Occasionally haughty about cuisine, but open to watching food television programs. Want to be appreciated for their bread-making abilities and for their high-quality olive oils.

41–50 points: KELLERIAN
Deep knowledge of gastronomy. Exhibit extraordinary finesse in all things culinary. Want harmony in their kitchen and work with determination to establish it. Skilled in all culinary arts, with a particular specialty in *sousvide*. Flexible and tolerant of the occasional lowbrow food (Skippy peanut butter), they take a pragmatic approach to cooking that is focused on results.

Acknowledgments

It goes without saying that I owe a tremendous debt of gratitude to two phenomenal "characters" in the world of food: Ruth Reichl and Anthony Bourdain. Never before have two fictional people felt so real, and they have both been so inspirational to me and to the writing of this important book. Whoever the secret masterminds are who are pulling their strings, I am deeply grateful.

I must acknowledge the enormous support of the many chefs and writers who through their encouragement, thoughtful insights, and occasional deep-tissue massages helped make this book possible. Mario Batali, in particular, deserves enormous praise for keeping my refrigerator stocked with cured meats throughout the writing process. I want to also thank Tom Colicchio, who kept me supplied with tangerine zest, read many of my earliest drafts, and kept my nails buffed to a wonderful shine using his beautiful bald head. Without Eric Ripert's support, his custom-made squid-ink hair dye, and his daily deliveries of *uni,* which kept me physically sustained for hours at my writing desk, this book would never have come to fruition. I am thankful for Tuscan butcher Dario Cecchini, whose gift of a steak-bone back scratcher was indispensable after an unfortunate foraging incident in Chianti involving poison ivy. I am so very grateful for Rick Bayless, who contributed his yoga techniques to this book and has been a wonderful friend, even if his breath smells like epazote. Writer Michael Ruhlman deserves my thanks for believing in me, proofreading my final drafts, and showing me the pleasures of "roasting a chicken." I also want to thank former *New York Times* restaurant critic Sam Sifton for sharing his personal list of food synonyms with me (he's a toothsome guy, that one). Speaking of chicken, I must extend my thanks to Jonathan Waxman, that master of poultry, who always spatchcocked when I needed it most. Where would I be without Thomas Keller, who butter-poached me into a relaxed state of mind when the stress of finishing this book was too great? Finally, I am thankful for my deep and abiding friendship with Jeremiah Tower, and especially for being my partner in crime as we toilet-papered Alice Waters's house one summer night in Berkeley when she annoyed the shit out of me.

It should be noted that there are also a number of people I am not grateful for whatsoever: Guy Fieri, Paula Deen, Rocco DiSpirito, Sandra Lee, Rachael Ray, and Gwyneth Paltrow.

I would, of course, like to thank everyone at Andrews McMeel, and in particular my editor, Dorothy O'Brien, for helping birth this baby. Few publishers would have the time, stamina, and emotional strength to encourage a home birth, but when I asked to give birth to this book at home in a tub filled with absinthe and foie gras, not only was Andrews McMeel totally encouraging, but they even footed the bill! I am also grateful to Jean Sagendorph, of the Mansion Street Literary Agency, for being my strongest advocate and doing whatever it takes—except for eating tortoise balls; she wouldn't do that—to make this lifelong project a reality.